ISSUE 22, OCTOBER 2024

AUSTRALIAN FOREIGN AFFAIRS

Contributors

Jacqui Baker is a principal fellow at the Indo-Pacific Research Centre at Murdoch University and a host of the podcast *Talking Indonesia*.

Damien Cave is Australia bureau chief at *The New York Times*, and the author of the memoir *Into the Rip: How the Australian Way of Risk Made my Family Stronger, Happier … and Less American.*

Priya Chacko is associate professor of international politics in the Department of Politics and International Relations at the University of Adelaide.

Carmen Lawrence is a former West Australian premier and a minister in state and federal governments. She is professor emerita in the School of Psychological Science at the University of Western Australia.

Connor O'Brien is a politics PhD student at the University of Cambridge.

Malcolm Turnbull was Prime Minister of Australia from 2015 to 2018.

Michael Wesley is deputy vice chancellor (Global, Culture and Engagement) and professor of politics at the University of Melbourne.

Australian Foreign Affairs is published three times a year by Australian Foreign Affairs Pty Ltd. Publisher: Morry Schwartz. Editor-in-chief: Erik Jensen. ISBN 978-1-76064-4338 ISSN 2208-5912 Subscriptions – 1 year print & digital auto-renew (3 issues): $49.99 within Australia incl. GST. 1 year print and digital subscription (3 issues): $59.99 within Australia incl. GST. 2 year print & digital (6 issues): $114.99 within Australia incl. GST. 1 year digital only auto-renew: $29.99. Payment may be made by MasterCard, Visa or Amex, or by cheque made out to Schwartz Books Pty Ltd. Payment includes postage and handling. To subscribe, fill out the form inside this issue, subscribe online at www.australianforeignaffairs.com, email subscribe@australianforeignaffairs.com or phone 1800 077 514 / 61 3 9486 0288. Correspondence should be addressed to: The Editor, Australian Foreign Affairs, 22–24 Northumberland Street, Collingwood, VIC, 3066 Australia Phone: 61 3 9486 0288 / Fax: 61 3 9486 0244 Email: enquiries@australianforeignaffairs.com. Editor: Jonathan Pearlman. Deputy Editor: Julian Welch. Associate Editor: Chris Feik. Design: Peter Long. Production Coordination: Marilyn de Castro. Typesetting: Tristan Main. Printed in Australia by McPherson's Printing Group.

Editor's Note

THE BAD GUYS

In 2017, Australia released its third foreign policy white paper and – for the first time – outlined a set of values that the country seeks to promote on the international stage.

The inaugural white paper, in 1997, made no mention of values, and the 2003 paper, released as Australian troops were about to fight in the Iraq War, made a flag-waving reference to Australians valuing "tolerance, perseverance and mateship". In contrast, the 2017 paper declared full-throated support for "political, economic and religious freedoms, liberal democracy, the rule of law, racial and gender equality and mutual respect".

As the late Allan Gyngell noted, detailing these classically liberal values in a post-Trump, post-truth world sounded "remarkably radical" and was motivated by China's growing influence. But the document was also careful to send a message to China that Australia did not intend to impose these values on others and would limit itself to partnering with other regional democracies.

This approach appeared to survive Australia's change of government in May 2022. A day after he was elected, Prime Minister Anthony

Albanese flew to Tokyo to meet with the leaders of the Quad, which comprises Australia, Japan, India and the United States. In his first comments on the global stage, Albanese said: "Our cooperation is built on the values that we share. A commitment to representative democracy, the rule of law and the right to live in peace."

But this assumption – that Australia's partners, such as India and the United States, share a commitment to liberal democracy – is increasingly under threat.

Narendra Modi, India's prime minister, has been accused of suppressing critics and the opposition, and discriminating against Muslims and other minorities. According to democracy watchdogs, he has transformed the country into a "hybrid" system that is somewhere between a democracy and an autocracy. In the United States, Donald Trump threatens to interfere with electoral processes and the rule of law if he regains power. Other Australian partners have also been sliding away from democracy, including Indonesia, whose incoming president, Prabowo Subianto, is an ultranationalist with a dark past and authoritarian inclinations.

These trends could require Australia to change either its partners or its rhetoric. Almost certainly the rhetoric will bend. As China rises and regional tensions and anxieties increase, Australia is likely to cling more closely to its partners, even if it must compromise on its values.

But the challenge for Australia extends beyond potential shifts of rhetoric and principle – developments which many realists, at least, will readily accept. The illiberal turn among Australia's friends reflects changes in the way these countries view the world. The United States, India and Indonesia are large and powerful nations: changes in their self-conception have global implications. Their turn towards illiberalism is likely to be matched by foreign policies that are increasingly self-interested, nativist, inconsistent and suspicious of enemies, friends and multilateralism.

For a country such as Australia, which thrives in a rules-based order because it does not have the clout to independently make or break global rules, an illiberal turn among its friends poses dangerous risks. It will be crucial for Australia to examine and understand the nation-changing developments occurring among some of its closest partners. These countries' tremors are a concern not just for their citizens, but also for their friends.

Jonathan Pearlman

FATEFUL MIX

Great powers, strongman leaders and manifest destinies

Michael Wesley

The world that Australian statecraft must navigate is becoming less and less familiar to our strategic and diplomatic traditions. The international system, reassuringly unipolar at the dawn of the century, is steadily evolving towards tripolarity. American primacy has been effectively challenged and ended by the rise of China, but India is fast rising and will form the third pole of a triangular balance from the middle of the century. No other country has the scale, demographic weight, internal cohesion and self-belief necessary to rise to equivalence with these three.

A three-way balance between great powers of similar capabilities will be highly competitive and unstable. Each will dread the prospect of its two rivals making common cause against it, and so will be intensely focused on containing its bilateral antagonism with each, while ensuring that distrust between its rivals remains substantial.

The competition and instability will likely be exacerbated by a trend that has emerged in the international arena over the past two decades, which has seen a different type of leader rise to power in country after country. This is a leader who dominates their country in a way conventional presidents and prime ministers don't. A leader who is driven by a sense of absolute self-belief as the saviour who will return the nation to its true nature and destiny, who rejects established elites and institutions, and who promises to attain or restore national greatness. A leader whose image, voice and thoughts are dominant and ubiquitous, and whose adversaries struggle to cut through.

When such leaders control great powers, they tend to magnify their country's great-power obsessions and tendencies. In such a world, all other nations, whether rivals or allies, must anticipate the fallout and be ready to adapt.

The rise of charismatic leaders

A century ago, the great German sociologist Max Weber discussed an outlier variant of leadership that emerges in times of "psychic, physical, economic, ethical, religious, political distress". He called this style of leadership "charismatic" and outlined its essence:

> The holder of charisma seizes the task that is adequate for him and demands obedience and a following by virtue of his mission ... he does not derive his "right" from [his followers'] will,

> in the manner of an election. Rather, the reverse holds: it is the duty of those to whom he addresses his mission to recognise him as their charismatically qualified leader.

For observers such as the *Financial Times*' Gideon Rachman, the world has entered "the age of the strongman". He charts the rise of a series of leaders, including Vladimir Putin, Recep Tayyip Erdoğan, Xi Jinping, Narendra Modi, Viktor Orbán, Jarosław Kaczyński, Boris Johnson, Donald Trump, Rodrigo Duterte and Jair Bolsonaro. He sees strong similarities and affinities among these leaders and repeatedly raises the peril they pose to liberal democracy. Others, too, have found a rich seam for comparative analysis here. Essays on populism, rising illiberalism and democratic backsliding are filling an ever greater number of pages in academic journals with each passing year.

Much of this commentary reflects its authors' deep attachments to liberal, internationalist and rationalist ideals, and their alarm at the rise and seeming invincibility of figures such as Putin, Modi and Erdoğan. What is often overlooked are the conditions that favour the rise of charismatic leaders, the advantages and techniques of charismatic leadership, and its effect on societies and states. As 2024 concludes, we may find that these are crucial questions for Australia, because charismatic leaders could by then be in charge of (or poised to assume power in) the four most important countries to Australia's future: India, China, Indonesia and the United States.

The chemistry of charisma

Charisma in politics is both a calling and a technique; it is not necessarily, as in general parlance, an innate talent. Leaders such as Vladimir Putin and Xi Jinping are not renowned for their looks, humour or charm, but they have been highly successful in developing the techniques of charismatic leadership.

Charismatic leaders stand out because they reject the constraints of conventional leadership. Conventional leaders are the product of institutionalised political machines. They are hyper-aware of the precarity of their power, cautious in their assessment of what they can achieve, risk-averse in what they say publicly, respectful of the status quo, and incrementalist in their forays into policy.

Charismatic leaders shatter this mould. They see the paradigm of conventional leadership as a symptom of the problems they have been called to solve. They invoke a sense of lost national greatness, squandered by the venality and self-interest of cosmopolitan elites and their allies in the "deep state". Driven by a sense of destiny, they see themselves as society's salvation against existential threats. They identify with and attempt to personify a cultural essence of the nation, which, they claim, is being strangled, corrupted or diluted by internal forces working in tandem with malign external influences. Donald Trump's inaugural address in 2017 offers a prime example of this thinking:

> For too long, a small group in in our nation's capital has reaped the rewards of government while the people have borne the

> cost. Politicians prospered – but the jobs left, and the factories closed … Mothers and children trapped in poverty in our inner cities; rusted-out factories scattered like tombstones across the landscape of our nation; an education system flush with cash, but which leaves our young and beautiful students deprived of knowledge; and the crime and gangs and drugs that have stolen too many lives and robbed our country of so much potential.

Charismatic leaders are highly sensitive to criticism and will go to any lengths to avoid being seen as weak or not in control, while accusing their opponents of precisely those qualities. They pursue what political scientist M. Steven Fish defines as "high dominance" leadership strategies:

> High-dominance leaders shape reality. They embrace conflict, chafe at playing defence and exhibit self-assurance even in pursuit of popular goals. By contrast, low-dominance leaders accept reality as it is and shun conflict. They tell people what they think they want to hear and prefer mollification to confrontation.

The opening decades of this century have been highly conducive to the emergence of charismatic leaders across countries diverse in geography, development and political systems. Rapid change and perceptions of economic, cultural or demographic insecurity prime the public for appeals to a return to traditional values and forceful solutions. A recent Ipsos survey of twenty-eight countries found that

58 per cent of respondents thought their country is in decline; 57 per cent felt that their country is broken; and 62 per cent had negative feelings towards elites. Consequently, 63 per cent of respondents felt their country needs a strong leader to reclaim it from the rich and powerful.

Charismatic playbooks

Modern politics is being transformed by the discovery of the power of emotions. Evoking fear, contempt, hope or anger is increasingly more effective than appeals to rationality, self-interest or the public good. Parties and candidates are appealing to voters' hearts rather than their heads, and to their "gut" rather than their hip pocket. These techniques are guided by advances in behavioural sciences that have increased our understanding of people's cognitive biases and reliance on intuition over reasoning.

Charismatic leaders harness emotions – about fear of change, anger at elites, pride in cultural greatness and yearning for future greatness – to build and consolidate their power and connect with their followers. Appeals to loyalty, authenticity and tradition are used to delegitimise established, globalised elites and create a sense that the leader's cause is existential.

Technology has given charismatic leaders another means of building connection and emotional engagement. Modi, Trump and Indonesia's Prabowo Subianto are masters in the use of social media to generate a constant dialogue with millions of supporters. Indeed, Modi has gone even further, using holograms of himself to address audiences. Social media disintermediates older forms of political communication and mobilisation, such as political parties, the traditional media and institutions such as parliaments. Its system of "likes" and "dislikes" creates a parallel, instant and constant form of democracy, demonstrating the appeal of a leader or an idea through numbers of followers, likes and re-postings. And its ecology fosters hyper-emotionalism by ensuring that the outrageous goes viral while the reasonable remains obscure.

Weber wrote that the greatest challenge faced by charismatic leaders is to overcome the transience of their power. Leadership based on emotional appeals, grand claims and an image of omnipotence is vulnerable to the short attention spans, mistakes and frustrations that are integral to politics. Consequently, techniques designed to perpetuate charismatic leaders' power and dominance are crucial.

Cultivating celebrity is a must. Charismatic leaders curate and promote their own life story, typically framing it as a rise from obscurity to greatness, called by destiny. Even those such as Xi Jinping, who was born to privilege, emphasise a fall (in Xi's case, being exiled to the countryside during the Cultural Revolution), followed by a subsequent rise. Modi's origins as the son of a tea-seller are the basis on which he connects to ordinary Indians, and form a contrast with the privileged Nehru/Gandhi dynasty that dominates the opposition Congress Party. Privileged from birth, Trump emphasises his outsider status to connect with his base. The 13 July 2024 assassination attempt offered him an ideal opportunity to burnish his outsider, tough-guy image. These and other charismatic leaders create a parallel between their own destiny and their nation's destiny. The personalisation of power is the route to political dominance: the leader's persona often overshadows the party they lead. Their objective is to fuse loyalty to the nation with loyalty to the leader; they aim to become the embodiment of the society they dominate. Supporters are encouraged to believe that only the leader can deliver national salvation and greatness.

A second defence against transience is to try to transform the state and society in the charismatic leader's image. Institutions that critique or stymie the exercise of power – such as the media, universities and the judiciary – are sidelined, cowed, co-opted or controlled. Charismatic leaders in democracies assiduously try to shift the electoral dynamics in their favour: in Prabowo's case, by using social media to galvanise young voters; in Modi's, by creating powerful messages of Hindu solidarity that can overcome caste, class and regional loyalties and align the 80 per cent of India's population who are Hindu behind him. Trump has remoulded the Republican Party in his image. In non-democratic China, Xi has elevated and empowered the Communist Party to infiltrate all institutions and facets of society in order to ensure broad compliance with the Supreme Leader's will.

A significant challenge is to maintain a perpetually activated support base. For charismatic leaders, the campaigning never stops. Political life becomes an unending series of causes, controversies and mobilisations that connect the leader to their supporters. Here, jarring the sensibilities of their liberal opponents is a tried and tested technique. By provoking outrage and denunciation from liberals, charismatic leaders keep their supporters permanently activated against those who loathe (and are loathed by) their leader. Charismatic leaders and their supporters expect absolute loyalty; those who seem less than fully committed are rounded on and cast aside.

Charismatic leaders are also revolutionary communicators, unconstrained by traditional considerations of probity or civility. In the Philippines, Rodrigo Duterte's expletive-laden rants, far from alienating the electorate, helped burnish his tough-guy persona. Charismatic leaders promise simple, emotionally satisfying solutions to complex problems, and take pride in brushing aside the complexities and costs of their programs. Unlike conventional leaders, who rely on highly institutionalised parties to deliver them power, charismatic leaders often favour grassroots campaigning, seeking through social media and volunteers to connect their message to people en masse.

Cold monsters

Friedrich Nietzsche called the state "the coldest of cold monsters". History shows there is an even colder variant: great powers, states that subsume the interests of other states into their own global interests. The more powerful they become, the more vulnerable they feel, and the stronger grows their sense of special providence and destiny. The rise of charismatic leaders to lead these colder monsters could well create the coldest variant of all.

Great powers are animated by an assiduously cultivated sense of exceptionalism. The belief that they are different from and superior to other societies justifies their extent, their power and their claims on other countries. Their exceptionalism is fed by a moral narrative that combines origins and destiny in a way that explains the imperative of wielding great power, their responsibilities in maintaining it and their justification in using it against others. Power and self-belief lead to a worldview structured according to a sense of material and moral hierarchy.

Charismatic leaders curate and promote their own life story

The American moral narrative stems from the Pilgrim Fathers' certainty that they were God's elect, and the Founding Fathers' belief that they were creating a society of perfect freedom and democracy. China's narrative draws on the cultural and ideological depth of its own civilisation to develop a sense that it is superior to the dominant West. Independent India has had two moral narratives: an original Gandhian/Nehruvian exceptionalism drawing on the independence struggle's non-violent ethics, and a new variant inspired by an interpretation of Hindu history, culture and ethics. Indonesia's exceptionalism is more limited and regional: it draws on pride in pre-colonial empires that have dominated South-East Asia, and manifests in its self-image as the leading contemporary power in that region.

The arrival of charismatic leaders in all four of these states has transformed the nature of their exceptionalism. Trump rejected the universalism that came with American exceptionalism, claiming that the United States has no special mission to spread its values to other societies but must assert its interests just as other states assert theirs. Xi draws on China's Confucian and classical culture more heavily than any other leader of the People's Republic has, and claims that China is redefining the nature of being a great power, away from hegemonism, exploitation and aggression. The Bharatiya Janata Party began to move India away from the Gandhian/Nehruvian conception of exceptionalism in the late 1990s. Nuclear tests in 1998 signalled its shift towards a more conventional great power identity; under Modi's leadership, this has become infused with a Hindu exceptionalism. It is too early to tell how Prabowo will interpret Indonesia's exceptionalism. There is a strong possibility he might seek to distinguish himself from his predecessor, Joko Widodo, who, as Indonesianist Eve Warburton observes, models himself on President Suharto, by drawing on the older, more expansive tradition of President Sukarno.

The paradox of great powers is that the more powerful they become, the more vulnerable they feel. Their sense of vulnerability is twofold. On the one hand, they are hyper-aware of the history of great powers, and the ultimate transience of their power. Consequently, part of their self-belief is a conviction that they are a uniquely different great power: the only one in history that can escape the cycle of rise and fall, thanks to the exceptional nature of their society. On the other hand, they are convinced that others are jealous of their position and privileges and are working to undermine or diminish their standing. Often great powers' behaviour, driven by the imperative of counteracting these insecurities, has the effect of motivating others to resist and undermine their power, which in turn feeds their insecurities.

An exaggerated sense of vulnerability leads great powers to expand the definition of security that motivates their statecraft. Beyond worrying about physical threats, they become increasingly preoccupied by normative dangers: situations in the world that appear to imperil the ideals that animate their societies. During and after the Cold War, the United States associated its security with the adoption of American-aligned freedoms, democracy and capitalism in other societies. China worries about the corrosive effects of these values – in particular, American-inflected demands for freedoms – on its regime and societal stability. Both seek to defend their societal values while working abroad to undermine the legitimacy and influence of values they oppose.

Charismatic leaders are masters of the narrative of threat and virility. Xi has used a familiar trope – corruption within, subversion from without – to position himself as the deliverer of redemption for the authentic China. His anti-corruption campaign has eliminated many of the domestic challenges to his authority, while his statecraft is ostensibly directed at reforming the nature of international relations towards China's ideals of harmony and mutual benefit. To other countries in its region, this can appear as belligerence and uncompromising insistence on Beijing's preferences. Modi speaks to India's Hindus as historically downtrodden and threatened by externally imposed religions, institutions and agendas such as secularism and affirmative action. His own vigour and virility are portrayed as leading the rise and development of an authentically Hindu India. Trump's variation on the theme of threat and virility turns on the danger of infiltration by undesirable immigrants, and exploitation by ruthless competitors and allies abroad. Only he has the toughness and guile to counter these threats.

The growth of a state's power has important consequences for its tolerance of perceived threats. Political commentator Robert Kagan illustrates the perceptual effect of different levels of power using a simple parable:

> A man armed only with a knife may decide that a bear prowling the forest is a tolerable danger, inasmuch as the alternative – hunting the bear armed only with a knife – is actually riskier than lying low and hoping the bear never attacks. The same man armed with a rifle, however, will likely make a different calculation of what constitutes a tolerable risk. Why should he risk being mauled to death if he doesn't have to?

Great powers tend to have low tolerance for situations they see as threatening or even undesirable, and a tendency to overestimate their ability to influence or control situations beyond their borders. They can be impatient with states, institutions or norms that they see as stymying their priorities, and have little compunction in frustrating other states' interests in pursuit of their own. There is a strong tendency among great powers to underestimate risk and to assume others want the same outcome they do.

Closely related to great powers' impatience with interests or considerations other than their own is a heightened sense of national honour and an acute sensitivity to insult and criticism. Highly attuned to their reputation, great powers tend to conflate the ends and means of statecraft, investing in values such as influence, access and credibility as objectives in themselves. As the United States showed in Vietnam, Iraq and Afghanistan, great powers will continue to shoulder the material cost of a failing intervention in the interests of maintaining an intangible value such as credibility. Despite their claims to global interests, great powers are often solipsistic, paying more attention to events, perceptions and norms within their societies than to those beyond their borders. This can lead to assumptions that the rest of the world wants what they want, and surprise, anger and vindictiveness towards those who do not.

Fateful synergies

The rise of charismatic leaders to dominate the four countries most significant to Australia's future is a development to which it should pay close attention. There are deep synergies between how charismatic leaders think and campaign, and the particular tendencies manifested by great powers.

The conviction of exceptionalism is a point of connection between a charismatic leader and the great power they lead. The sense of a personal calling and the trajectory of a rise from humble beginnings feed a narrative of the leader as essential to the nation achieving and maintaining wealth, power and respect. Without the leader, the nation's exceptionalism is undermined by corrupt, self-serving, incompetent elites; it is only the charismatic leader's genius and virility that can banish these influences and allow national greatness to manifest. This synergy between the personal and collective senses of predestination is likely to exacerbate the great power's belief in its exceptionalism and magnify its consequences.

Exceptionalism can lead to an overestimation of a great power's capability to achieve what it wants in the world, especially when it is led by someone with a self-conception of unique potency. From Xi's grand "Belt and Road" vision to Trump's vow never to let North Korea develop nuclear weapons, charismatic leaders are inspired by their own sense of special calling and their country's exceptional nature to assume monumental tasks.

At the same time, the great power's worries about internal and external vulnerabilities provide constant opportunities for the charismatic leader to appear vigilant and resolute. Xi has heightened the public's sense of humiliation in relation to unresolved territorial disputes, allowing China to appear wronged and its opponents malign, and magnifying the prominence of his combative pronouncements and the assertive actions of the People's Liberation Army and Navy.

Modi reacted to a February 2019 terrorist attack in Jammu and Kashmir by directing air strikes into Pakistan; soon after, he adopted the Twitter handle "Chowkidar [watchman, guardian] Modi" and campaigned strongly on keeping India safe from internal and external threats. Trump's "American carnage" message, central to his inaugural address, continued through his presidency and beyond, allowing him to identify internal and external malevolent forces. His uncompromising, self-aggrandising rhetoric is intended to show that only he is tough enough to do what needs to be done to keep America safe. Prabowo's presidential campaigns in 2014 and 2019 were notable for the angry, rousing, nationalist and even xenophobic rhetoric used by the candidate. While he notably softened his image and language in 2024, few Indonesia watchers interpret this as little more than a temporary expedient to get himself elected.

A muscular approach to dealing with perceived threats is likely to be matched by hypersensitivity to criticism or disrespect. Charismatic leaders base their appeal on an image of virility and decisiveness, and consequently strive to avoid looking weak or hesitant. When in charge of great powers, they become highly protective of the nation's reputation and image abroad, reacting with prickly antagonism towards countries that are deemed to be insufficiently deferential. Under Xi, China has rounded on country after country that were said to have "hurt the feelings of the Chinese people". Trump's contempt for close US allies is based on his perception that they have exploited America's generosity, and therefore should be treated as free riders. Prabowo has repeatedly flirted with anti-Chinese stances, promoting the meme *asing den aseng*, which implies that Chinese Indonesians are aligned with the People's Republic and are attempting to colonise Indonesia economically.

Girt by three ... plus one

It is likely that the three states that will make up our tripolar world – the United States, China and India – will do what great powers usually do: seek to draw smaller states into their orbit, and create spheres of influence close to their own borders. These are ideally buffer zones of compliant societies, places in which other great powers judge it too risky to intervene.

The most important region in the tripolar competition is likely to be South-East Asia, plus the islands of New Guinea and Australia. This region sits between India and China and straddles the passages between the Pacific and Indian oceans. Its resource wealth and economic significance add to its geographical importance, making it of intense interest to all three great powers.

Here Indonesia stands out. It has the largest economy and population in South-East Asia and is the most strategically located country in the region, so how it positions itself assumes an ever greater importance. Its stance, and the nature of its ties with Delhi, Beijing and Washington, will have significant effects on the positions and opportunities open to its neighbours – including Australia.

How Australia positions itself in relation to the tripolar balance and Indonesia's stance will be the most important question its strategic policymakers have ever confronted. Australia's challenge – shared by all smaller powers during times of unstable multipolarity – is how to maximise its independence and capitalise on the opportunities created by great power competition, while also minimising the risks of that competition. Calibrating Canberra's bilateral relations with Delhi, Beijing, Washington and Jakarta to maximise Australia's independence and advantage and minimise its risk, while understanding how each of these bilaterals will affect the other bilaterals, demands sophistication and careful calculation. This is not something Canberra has ever had to do before.

The new strategic and diplomatic world Australia is entering will be contested by three roughly equivalent powers, and global and regional institutions and norms will be gradually weakened by that competition. This will demand a fundamental remaking of our strategic frameworks and reformulation of our statecraft, less clearly aligned to our great-power ally and its perceptions of international affairs, towards a more fine-grained and consistent focus on our own interests, advantages and vulnerabilities. It will require a much stronger and more historically informed understanding of the motivations and patterns of behaviour of great powers, regardless of their ideological or cultural identities. And Australia needs to become much better at anticipating the reactions and passions of those who will be drawn to lead this century's most powerful states: charismatic leaders, and their distinctive type of politics. ■

SECOND COMING

How to deal with Trump

Malcolm Turnbull

Blood streaming down his face, framed with a blue sky and an American flag, fist clenched in defiance – this is the indelible image of Donald Trump from this campaign, and perhaps for all time.

Moments after an assassin's bullet clipped his right ear, Trump showed real bravery under fire – literally – and had all his political wits about him. The Secret Service agents wanted to rush him away to safety. He told them to wait, and there he struck the hero's pose of courageous, unbending strength.

From that moment, on 13 July, Trump seemed unstoppable. It was the most extraordinary comeback. Only three and a half years ago, in the last days of his first term as president, he was inciting a mob to storm the Capitol and disrupt the constitutional transfer of power. His wild claims that the election had been stolen were echoed in sympathetic right-wing media outlets like Fox News, but rejected by every court in which they were tested.

And yet he has persuaded the vast majority of Republicans, and about a third of all Americans, that he is right. His insistence on this, his biggest lie, has become an article of faith to the Republican Party. Trump is the most audacious and successful gaslighter of our time.

But if a week is a long time in politics, a month is an eon. After a catastrophic debate on 27 June, followed by his own three weeks of gaslighting denials, Joe Biden finally pulled out of the race on 22 July – nine days after Trump's narrow brush with the would-be assassin.

Biden's vice president, Kamala Harris, has succeeded him as the Democratic candidate and has enjoyed an enormous relief rally, breaking every presidential campaign record for donations and volunteers. The race has tightened; she is ahead in some battleground polls. At fifty-nine, she has relative youth on her side, and she has chosen a warm, charismatic sixty-year-old white guy as her running mate: Tim Walz, the governor of Minnesota.

As I write this essay, there is momentum, energy and optimism around the Democratic campaign that has been lacking for years. But Harris is entering the contest late, the electorate is very polarised and most voters have made up their minds. The race is very close, the Electoral College favours Trump and polls have historically underestimated his support.

So, whether we like it or not, we are likely looking at another four years of President Donald Trump. And four years of Vice President J.D. Vance. Forty years old, the junior senator from Ohio has the perfect political backstory of triumph over a deprived upbringing, addicted mother and absent father – brilliantly described in his bestselling memoir, *Hillbilly Elegy*.

Eight years ago, Vance was comparing Trump to Adolf Hitler, but for the last four – and especially since Trump's endorsement got him elected in 2022 – he has been the chief acolyte. He has positioned himself to the right of Trump, as the younger version ready to keep the MAGA dream alive from 2028.

This time Trump will be determined to have his own way. The *soi-disant* "very stable genius" will be more confident than ever. Hasn't he beaten overwhelming odds, prosecutions, convictions, even an assassin's bullet? He will ride back into Washington like a conquering Caesar in his triumph – but there won't be a slave next to him in the chariot whispering, "Remember that you are mortal."

Trump has always been surrounded by yes men and sycophants – personalities like his attract them. The independent-minded either never join, don't stay or get fired. But this time he knows the ropes. He believes the Washington official establishment – what he calls the "deep state" – frustrated his agenda in his first term. He won't let that happen again, and he will have plenty of collaborators. Instead of well-meaning people of real experience like his defence secretary, General Jim Mattis, and secretary of state, Rex Tillerson, who did their best to provide "adult supervision" during Trump's first term, there is an army of MAGA zealots determined to support Trump's increasingly radical "conservative" agenda.

The Heritage Foundation, Washington's largest right-wing think tank, has worked with likeminded Trump supporters to coordinate "Project 2025", a detailed plan for a second Trump administration to replace most of the senior federal bureaucracy with Trump loyalists, abolish the Department of Education, deport all illegal immigrants, terminate all "diversity, equity and inclusion" (or DEI) programs and abolish environmental programs that support clean energy. Trump has tried to distance himself from it, but Project 2025 is thoroughly in line with his thinking, as his 93-minute acceptance speech to the Republican National Convention in Milwaukee, Wisconsin, in July 2024 demonstrated.

Take trade. Last time, Trump was determined to impose high tariffs to protect American industry, especially from China. In this he was supported by his advisers Peter Navarro and Robert Lighthizer, but most of his economic advisers – from Treasury secretary Steven Mnuchin to National Economic Council director Gary Cohn to son-in-law Jared Kushner – knew the plan would be self-defeating. They were able to moderate and delay much of Trump's agenda. Now he will have a team that is fully signed up to his vision.

The 2024 election is all about culture and ideology

Trump has promised an additional 60 per cent tariff on all Chinese imports, and an additional 10 per cent tariff on imports from all other countries. Apart from its obvious inflationary impacts, a unilateral tariff like this will provoke a response – just as his last round of tariff-setting did. Trump is foreshadowing not just a ramp-up of the existing trade war against China but a new trade war against trade itself.

Or take defence. Last time Trump came close to pulling out of NATO. He believed, as he had for years, that the Europeans were taking advantage of the United States and were freeloaders. Wiser heads prevailed – but will they be there next time?

What about Ukraine? At Trump's request, the Republicans in Congress held up US$60 billion of aid to Ukraine for six months – a delay Russian president Vladimir Putin ruthlessly exploited. Trump has said he will end the war "in a day". Few doubt that this can mean anything other than compelling Ukraine to accept large territorial concessions to Russia. Much of his MAGA base prefer Putin, and Trump's own admiration for the Russian dictator is palpable.

Trump's running mate, J.D. Vance, is unequivocal about the United States ending its military support for Ukraine; he voted against the April 2024 aid package. He is on the same page as Hungary's prime minister, Viktor Orbán, another Trump favourite, and advocates a negotiated peace with Putin. Earlier this year, he told the Munich Security Conference: "I do not think that Vladimir Putin is an existential threat to Europe, and to the extent that he is, again that suggests Europe has to take a more aggressive role in its own security."

On energy and climate, Trump will again pull out of the Paris Climate Agreement, scrap as many environmental regulations as he can, end support for electric vehicles, and promote gas guzzlers, coal and gas burning and exploration – a position summed up by his promise for his first day: "Drill, baby, drill!" Many of the clean energy projects supported by Biden's *Inflation Reduction Act* are in "red" or Republican states, but that might not be enough to save them. The 2024 election, and Trump's MAGA movement more broadly, is all about culture and ideology. Not even economic self-interest will be able to resist it.

Now that we know what to expect, how should Australia contend with a second coming of Trump? Many in Canberra will say, and will want to believe, that nothing has changed. That our "hundred years of mateship", the ANZUS alliance and our mutual affection for Greg Norman will ensure that nothing bad happens and we can ride out the four years of Trump 2.0 without undue inconvenience.

Well, they might, but they probably won't. Trump is unlike any other president of modern times. He is not committed to democracy or the rule of law in the way most people understand it. His conduct on 6 January 2021 is proof enough of that, as is his affection for authoritarian leaders – not only the illiberal Orbán in Hungary and Putin in Russia, but also President Xi Jinping of China and, most improbably, North Korea's Kim Jong-un, who, Trump has told us, missed him and looked forward to renewing their friendly relationship. "It's nice to get along with someone who has a lot of nuclear weapons," he said.

Trump's view of the world is dystopian – think of his "American carnage" speech in 2017, on the occasion of his inauguration as president. A few months after that, when he and I met in New York, he summarised his views on East Asia: "The Chinese hate the Japanese, the Japanese hate the Koreans, the Koreans hate the Chinese and the Japanese, who also hate the Chinese." He was no different on the Middle East: "They all want to kill each other."

In Trump's mind, the rest of the world, including close allies, are sponging off the United States – not pulling their weight in defence spending and "unfairly" competing on trade. His slogan "America First" revived the name of the isolationist political movement that campaigned to keep America out of World War II. At one point led by the Nazi-sympathising aviator Charles Lindbergh, the America First Committee had 800,000 members; its ranks included many who admired the European fascists.

This isolationist tradition is alive and well in America today and Trump is channelling it. He has condemned the "forever wars" the old Republican Party embarked on in the Middle East. He is not a warmonger and does not believe in "nation building", and on foreign policy is the polar opposite of the Republican neoconservatives of the George W. Bush and Dick Cheney era.

While many in Washington are obsessed with the expansion of Chinese strategic and military power, Trump is more focused on Chinese economic power and the enormous trade surplus it has with the United States. It is far from clear that Trump would be prepared to fight to defend Taiwan – unlike Biden, he has never said that he would. Why would he want to defend democracy abroad when his commitment to it at home is, at best, highly conditional? In July, speaking to Bloomberg Businessweek, Trump came close to confirming that his administration would not defend Taiwan. He pointed to the practical difficulties of doing so: "Taiwan is 9500 miles away. It's 68 miles away from China." He said that Taiwan "took our chip business from us. I mean, how stupid are we?" Further, Taiwan is "immensely wealthy" and so should be paying the United States for protection. "I don't think we're any different from an insurance policy. Why? Why are we doing this?"

He admires President Xi, and says that if he were Xi he would take advantage of America too. Trump was very impressed, he once told me, by Xi's account of Chinese history, the centuries of humiliation by foreign powers, and by how Xi was making China great again. But he has no concerns about how tyrants such as Putin, Xi or Kim treat their own citizens, or even their neighbours, unless it impacts American interests. When Putin's invasion of Ukraine was going well, Trump described him as a genius. There is no moral dimension to Trump's view of the world – he assumes that everyone is ruthlessly acting in their own interests and will do whatever they can get away with.

It made a kind of sense, therefore, that Trump was introduced in Milwaukee by former wrestling champion Hulk Hogan and by Dana White, president of the Ultimate Fighting Championship. In Trump world, only strength and power matter.

Trump probably won't target Australia as an ungrateful, freeloading ally. America has a healthy trade surplus with Australia, although that is unlikely to protect us from a universal additional 10 per cent tariff on all imports to the United States. But while there is plenty of goodwill for Australia in Washington DC today, there is not a lot of leverage or agency.

The AUKUS deal has considerably reduced Australia's ability to make independent foreign-policy decisions. Our sovereignty is diminished. Thanks to the Morrison and Albanese governments, Australia is now more dependent on the United States than ever, right at the time the United States is likely to become less dependable than ever.

And the risk goes beyond Trump. The zeitgeist in Washington has changed. "America First" is a Trump slogan but it sums up a national mood of heightened self-interest. AUKUS means that American interests and priorities will always prevail over Australia's – or, put another way, that Washington will decide what's good for Australian defence, not Canberra.

AUKUS was announced on 15 September 2021. Scott Morrison cancelled the partnership with France to build a fleet of conventionally powered submarines in Adelaide using the design for France's latest nuclear-powered submarine. So far, Australia has committed to spend about $10 billion to support the US and UK submarine construction industries, as well as comparable amounts to establish a submarine base in Perth to be used by the US Navy's submarines.

The diplomatic drama around Morrison's deception of France overshadowed a major strategic departure, one that diminished Australia's sovereignty at precisely the wrong time. Morrison justified the cancellation of the French deal on the basis that our navy needed nuclear-powered submarines. But he never explained why he had not explored nuclear propulsion with France. Given just twenty-four hours to consider the radical shift, Anthony Albanese's Labor Opposition went along with the new plan, determined to avoid being wedged by Morrison on national security.

The long-term big idea was to partner with the United Kingdom to design and build nuclear-powered submarines (SSNs), using, as the Royal Navy does now, US nuclear-propulsion technology. But the United Kingdom has not yet completed the construction of two of its planned seven SSNs – the Astute class – and it has to build four new SSBNs (ballistic missile nuclear submarines), the Dreadnought class. The new AUKUS SSN has not yet been fully designed, and will not appear, at least for Australia, until the early 2040s – and that's if everything goes well, which would be highly unusual in such a large and complex defence project. The six boats of our existing submarine fleet, the Collins class, are between twenty and thirty years old and approaching retirement. So how ought we fill the capability gap between the retirement of the Collins class and the arrival of the new AUKUS SSNs?

The solution arrived at is for the US Navy to sell Australia between three and five Virginia-class SSNs, the first of which will arrive in 2032 and the next two in 2035 and 2037. We can potentially acquire another two if the AUKUS SSNs are late (as they almost certainly will be). The first two are to be second-hand boats with at least twenty years' service left, and the others are to be new.

However, there is an important caveat: the AUKUS legislation passed earlier this year by the US Congress specifically states that submarines cannot be sold to Australia unless, 270 days beforehand, the president certifies to the Congress that their sale is consistent with US foreign policy and national security interests, and specifically it will not degrade the undersea capabilities of the US Navy.

How likely is that? Right now, the US Navy is at least seventeen Virginia-class boats short of the number it says it needs. The submarine building industry is unable to keep up the maintenance of its current fleet. At the same time, the industry is completing between 1.2 and 1.3 Virginia-class submarines a year. If it is to catch up, it needs to double that production rate.

The Virginia-class SSNs are the most valuable and survivable assets of the US Navy. As the Russians have learned in the Black Sea in recent years, surface vessels are more vulnerable to attack than ever. The Virginia SSNs, technically superior to their Chinese counterparts, are the key to the US Navy countering a Chinese attack on Taiwan.

To believe that a US president would release any of these vital assets to Australia, you have to believe that the rate of production will more than double over the next few years, or that the United States' rivalry with China is going to evaporate. Neither seems likely.

The risk of an American president, or the Congress itself, concluding that the needs of the US Navy come first has been borne entirely by Australia. It is in the legislation. And several defence strategists in the Trump camp, such as Elbridge Colby, have been saying bluntly that it is just not realistic to expect the US Navy to diminish its own fleet at a time when they believe a naval war with China is a real and imminent possibility.

This decision may not be one that is made on Trump's watch, of course. Unless he can find a way to serve a third term, he would be out of office in January 2029, several years before the call has to be made. But if he did have to consider it, why would he do anything other than put "America First"?

The bully despises those people he suborns, while he respects those he cannot

And there is nothing we can do about it – with Trump at the helm, we would have to brace for his demand for additional payments to offset the expense of American submarines rotating in and out of the Perth base. Our utter, helpless, increased dependency on the United States will hardly inspire respect from Trump. We will be lucky if he can manage to hide his bemusement as to why we sent billions to support the US submarine industry without any assurance of getting a US submarine. You don't win respect from a New York property developer by doing dumb deals.

The more likely outcome has been flagged by the US Congress Research Service as "the US–Australia military division of labour". Under this alternative, Australia would not acquire any nuclear-powered submarines – the US Navy would rotate four to five SSNs out of Perth for both US and Australian purposes, and in return Australia would invest in other capabilities, such as drones, missiles or B-1 bombers, which would be likewise available for both US- and Australian-directed missions. Bottom line: no subs.

So how should Australia respond? And, more precisely, how should our mild-mannered prime minister deal with the bombastic bully in the White House?

First, Albanese will have to do the heavy lifting himself. There is a long list of would-be Trump whisperers, American and Australian, who will offer to help. Not all of them are grifters. They will all have contacts who claim to be close to Trump; a few might even be close to Trump themselves. But as I found out, the only way to get something done with Trump is by dealing with him directly.

In a normal government or administration, there is a system of officials and advisers with whom a foreign government can engage. Issues can be worked out at official levels. By the time they reach the desk of the president or the prime minister, they have essentially been resolved.

Trump is not like that. In his White House, there was only one decision-maker and that was Donald J. Trump. Of course, he had advisers and officials, but he didn't read their briefings and most of them didn't last long anyway.

Last time, Trump's election came as a surprise – even to him. Almost everyone had expected Hillary Clinton to win, and so in

November 2016 governments around the world were scrambling to work out how to deal with him.

Two big assumptions were generally made about Trump in 2016. The first proved to be wrong and won't be made again. The second was also wrong but will certainly be repeated.

The first mistake was to assume that Trump in office would be very different to Trump on the campaign trail. I was at the Asia-Pacific Economic Cooperation (APEC) meeting in November 2016, shortly after the US election, and all the leaders there were consoling themselves with variants of Mario Cuomo's line: "We campaign in poetry; you govern in prose." Not, as Chile's Michelle Bachelet observed, that there had been much poetry in the brutal campaign just concluded.

Even hardheads like President Xi were optimistic. The Chinese leader was relaxed about Trump, confident the US governmental system would institutionalise him. The wild rhetoric was just for the campaign trail, he believed, and the colourful businessman would, once in the Oval Office, become a more conventional US president. We saw how that worked out. Trump in office was, if anything, wilder and more erratic than he'd been on the hustings.

The second assumption was that the only way to get on with Trump was to suck up to him – to use the approach Disraeli once recommended for royalty – lots of flattery, laid on with a trowel.

While I had several friends and business connections in common with Trump, I had never met him before I became prime minister. But I knew his type. He was, and remains, very much the big, bullying billionaire personality, like Kerry Packer, Robert Maxwell, Jimmy Goldsmith, Alan Bond, Conrad Black, Rupert Murdoch (to some extent) and many others. This type is narcissistic, driven, totally focused on accumulating wealth and power for themselves.

The one thing I had learned about this type of personality is that if you suck up to bullies or give in to them, the only thing you will get is more bullying. Punching them in the nose (metaphorically or actually) is rarely successful either. To succeed with them, you need to stand up to them – but courteously. The only thing they respect is strength. The bully despises those people he suborns, while he respects (even if he does not like) those he cannot.

My inclination as to how to deal with Trump was quite different from the sort of pop psychology advice that was current in government circles: "flatter him", "talk about golf" and so on. Circumstances quickly put my theory to the test.

In 2016 I had agreed with President Barack Obama that the United States would resettle up to 1500 asylum seekers who were then detained on Manus Island, in Papua New Guinea, and Nauru. These were people who had sought to come to Australia on boats with people smugglers and, for the most part, had been intercepted in 2013, when the second Rudd government sought to switch Australia's border-protection policy back to the hardline policies adopted by the Howard government. It was not a one-way deal – Australia also agreed to resettle some difficult cases for the Americans – but there was no doubt that Obama both understood our tough line on people smuggling and wanted to assist as many of the detained individuals as he could.

Once Trump was elected in November, we were concerned to ensure that the new administration upheld the bargain. Trump had campaigned on a platform of being tough on migration and proceeded to freeze the US refugee program, as well as impose bans on migration from several large Muslim-majority countries.

We sought and obtained assurances from Trump's team that they would stick to the deal, in recognition of the importance of the US–Australia relationship. And when the executive order banning refugees from certain Muslim countries was published, an express provision allowed the admission of otherwise prohibited refugees if "admitting the person would enable the United States to conform its conduct to a pre-existing international agreement". That augured well, we thought.

But then, just before a scheduled call with the new president, Foreign Minister Julie Bishop was called by Vice President Mike Pence, while my national security adviser, Justin Bassi, was called by his counterpart, General Mike Flynn. Both delivered the same message: President Trump had changed his mind. He wouldn't under any circumstances honour the deal, and the Australian prime minister should not mention the matter in the call.

Well, I did mention it, and the new president was most unhappy. He insisted it was a bad deal and that it would kill him politically if he honoured it. I replied that he was like a new CEO who inherits a bad deal from his predecessor: he can complain and bitch about it, but he must still honour it. The conversation became very heated when Trump said that I must have reneged on deals when I was in business. No, I said, I was a man of my word.

Trump was furious but could not argue further. Having begun the call as an emphatic no, he ended it as a most unhappy and reluctant yes. "I have no choice but to honour a deal made by my predecessor," he said. "I totally disagree with the deal, it's a horrible deal, a disgusting deal ... It's an embarrassment to the United States of America." Just before he terminated the call, he added: "This is the most unpleasant call I've had all day. Putin was a pleasant call."

Still, we weren't sure that he would honour the deal. I wanted to keep the call confidential, but Trump's team were quickly briefing the media about how angry he had been, even to the extent of leaking a (somewhat redacted) transcript of the call – all to demonstrate that the president had gone along with the deal with great reluctance.

The next time we met was in May 2017, on the USS *Intrepid*, an old aircraft carrier in New York. It was three months since the incandescent phone call. Jared Kushner, Trump's son-in-law, reminded me that it had been "a very bad call" and urged me to be low-key and deferential. He said his father-in-law "hadn't expected you to come on so strong, although we knew that was your reputation".

When Trump and I met, I didn't bring up the refugee deal, and it didn't come up until Melania and Lucy joined us. Trump turned to his wife and said, "Melania, do you know, Malcolm has two thousand of the worst terrorists in the world locked up on a desert island, and that fool Obama agreed to take them. Can you believe that? And now Malcolm has talked me into taking them too. He got me to do something I promised never to do. He is a tough negotiator!"

Melania replied, with a smile as faint as it was mischievous, "Just like you, Donald."

So it was just another deal. Trump could have been complaining that I had persuaded him to pay too much for a building in Brooklyn. It seemed surreal at the time, but the refugee deal stuck and many of those asylum seekers were settled in the United States. It was clear to me when we met on the *Intrepid* that standing up to Trump over the refugee deal had incurred his anger in the short term but his respect in the long term.

Someone had told him I'd represented Kerry Packer years ago, a fact Trump came back to at every meeting until it became almost a routine. "Malcolm is the best lawyer in the world, he kept my friend Kerry Packer out of jail," he would say.

"That's very kind, Donald," I'd reply, "but it wasn't that hard. He was innocent."

"Oh no," said Trump with a big grin, "he was so guilty, deserved to go to jail forever."

Jokes aside, I sensed that Trump liked knowing lawyers who had kept billionaires (innocent or not) out of jail. And the respect I had won would be of immense value to Australia when the next big issue arose.

By mid-2017, Trump was proposing to impose a 25 per cent tariff on steel imported to the United States, and 10 per cent on aluminium. The steel tariff was of great concern to BlueScope, which exported about 300,000 tonnes a year to California, where it was made into Colorbond roofing products by the company's American subsidiary. This was a tiny percentage of America's steel imports but very important to BlueScope and its Port Kembla workforce.

And for me there was a big principle at stake. Australia had, in John Howard's time, signed a free trade agreement with the United States that was, frankly, a better deal for America than it was for us. But the upshot was that there were no tariffs on American imports to Australia. Moreover, the United States had a substantial trade surplus with Australia.

Getting an exemption for Australia from Trump's tariffs was not easy and was only achieved by direct discussions with him. Our diplomats recommended some form of capitulation or compromise at every turn, and I don't blame them for that. "You have to give something to Trump," our ambassador to the United States, my former Liberal Party colleague Joe Hockey, would say.

Trump listened to my explanation of the economics of Australian steel exports. I told him that BlueScope exported steel to California at US$40 a tonne, compared to US$100 a tonne from the Midwest or East Coast steelmakers. We estimated that if the tariff was imposed, there would be no benefit to US steelmakers, just higher costs for roofing steel in California and substitution with non-steel roofing products. As a property developer, he understood this – he even recognised the

Colorbond product. "We used the gold-coloured one in some of our own projects. They really loved it in Brooklyn," he told me.

Ultimately, I was able to persuade him that it was not in his interests to impose the tariff on Australia. If his argument was that America was being ripped off by unfair trade deals with other countries, how could he impose tariffs on Australia?

"No tariffs, no quotas and a US$25-billion trade surplus," I said to him. "Truth be told, you have the best possible trade deal ever with Australia."

What does this mean for Albanese? He will be told to kiss Trump's arse and everybody in the Trump universe will encourage him to do it. Albanese needs the confidence to be warm but professional, courteous but utterly disciplined in defending his nation's interests – which may come as a surprise in Washington, given Australia's recent history.

Albanese will need to set the context and expectations for dealing with Trump. He should not conceal the fact that there are elements of Trump's agenda with which we disagree – on climate, trade and, potentially, Ukraine, just to begin with.

Trump is, now more than ever, a key part of the right-wing "angertainment" universe, the largest part of which is owned by Rupert Murdoch, whose media is enthusiastically promoting Trump and slamming Kamala Harris. So an Australian prime minister who finds himself at odds with Trump, regardless of the issue, should expect that Murdoch's media will side with Trump. This is why it is vital for

Albanese to make it clear that while the United States and Australia are strong allies and good friends, we do not always agree and our interests do not always align.

If Albanese stands up to Trump and is seen to disagree with him on certain issues, he will be attacked by both the right-wing media and the Opposition, who will say that Labor cannot get along with our most important ally. On the other hand, if he looks like a sycophant, the criticism will be that he is too weak to stand up for Australia. Either way, there will be no bouquets for Albanese in the right-wing media this close to an election – on foreign policy or anything else.

This is another reason to make sure his relationship with Trump gets off on the right foot. I wouldn't recommend a blazing row (that's a bit too high-risk even for me, let alone for Albanese), but it would be a mistake for Albanese to allow himself to be portrayed as "a mate" or to get too close to Trump. The relationship should be courteous, professional but above all businesslike.

Trump has double-crossed or fallen out with most people with whom he has been connected. The disappointment and humiliation if (when) Trump turns against Albanese will be much greater if the media have previously gushed about how close they are. In other words, keep smiling but keep some distance. Trump, after all, will act in what he regards as his own best interests. Look at all the grovelling and backslapping Boris Johnson engaged in with Trump. Did he secure the comprehensive free trade deal with America that he had promised would come with Brexit? Not a chance.

And what about Kevin Rudd, our present ambassador in Washington? A few months ago, the British populist Nigel Farage interviewed Trump and said he'd been asked "by my friends at Sky News Australia" to share some criticisms Rudd had made of Trump before he became ambassador. Trump clearly had no idea who he was talking about, but reacted as desired by suggesting that Rudd would not be ambassador for long with views like that. The Murdoch media promptly started a mini campaign calling for Rudd to be sacked.

Rudd is well regarded in Washington on both sides of the aisle for his experience as PM and his expertise on China. His enemies are all in Australia. He won't have a relationship with Trump. No ambassador will. Joe Hockey was not on the critical calls I had with Trump, let alone in the one-on-one meetings. This is no reflection on Joe, who did go to great lengths to cultivate relations with the people in Trump's orbit. It's simply a fact that ambassadors aren't in the room when it really matters. If Australia has business to do with Trump, only the prime minister can seal the deal. Recalling Rudd would be seen by Trump, and everyone else, as a craven capitulation.

AUKUS poses a special problem for Albanese

AUKUS poses a special problem for Albanese. Because he has adopted a policy of the former Coalition government, he gets little or no credit for its successes but will be blamed for any disappointments, on the grounds that he bungled a great opportunity left him by his predecessors.

Albanese has already suffered a big hit to his political capital by losing an unwinnable referendum. He needs to be careful now that he does not get blamed for "losing the Virginias" that were never likely to be sold to us. Labor only went along with the AUKUS submarine plan to avoid being wedged on national security. That may yet prove to be as bad a political decision as it was a strategic one.

But beyond the problems of AUKUS, Trump, especially paired with Vance, is going to rattle America's allies. Haven't we all been working together to stand up to authoritarian regimes like China, Russia and North Korea? So how does it look when the leader of the free world doesn't care whether they are run by tyrants, and even boasts of his beautiful friendships with them? Backslapping simply won't do this time around. Australia and its leaders need to be as ruthlessly focused on Australia's national interest as Trump is on America's.

The leaders of America's friends and allies, including Australia, will be among the few who can speak truthfully to Trump. He can shout at them, embarrass them, even threaten them. But he cannot fire them. Their character, courage and candour may be the most important aid they can render to the United States, if there is a second age of Trump. ■

FORCING HISTORY

Prabowo and the new deal for Indonesia's elites

Jacqui Baker

Prabowo Subianto, Indonesia's president come 20 October, is many things. He is, at least for these last political moments, Indonesia's defence minister in the second-term Joko Widodo government. He is a three-time loser of earlier presidential runs: first as Megawati Sukarnoputri's vice-presidential candidate in 2009, and then, in bruising campaigns in 2014 and 2019, against Jokowi. To Widodo, Prabowo is the torchbearer for his legacy, a political frenemy who is indebted to him for his 2024 electoral success. To tens of millions of young Indonesian voters, he is the cuddly, anointed successor of the beloved President Jokowi, with a penchant for daggy TikTok moves. To a cohort of voters with much longer memories, he is the veteran of a brutal and oppressive military who has devoted three decades of public life to weaponising agitation and extrajudicial violence in service of his own political ambitions.

First and foremost, though, Prabowo Subianto should be understood as a blueblood. He is a Djojohadikusumo, a family best understood as fully paid-up members of an Indonesian "postcolonial class", a stratum of extremely wealthy, extremely powerful changeling families that are adept at maintaining their privilege across a range of political regimes. For the Djojohadikusumos, the pursuit of power has not been smooth and yet, in the face of missteps that for other elites might have proven fatal, this family has preserved and accumulated their social power, right up until 20 October, when the apex of political power – the presidency – will be in their hands.

Born to rule

Like most dynasties in postcolonial republics, the Djojohadikusumos are the perverse products of empire. The family's minor claim to Javanese gentry – the element "*kusumo*" in the name signals Javanese nobility – gave them entry into the Dutch civil service, which opened up channels of economic and political power. Prabowo's grandfather Margono grew up in East Java in a family that had aristocratic claims but was economically humble. Margono followed in his father's footsteps, progressing from a Dutch education to a career in the Dutch East Indies' department of the interior, specialising in banking. During the war for Indonesian independence, two of Margono's young sons were killed during a raid on a Japanese armoury for weapons, leaving only his eldest son, Sumitro – Prabowo's father. After independence, Margono established Bank Negara Indonesia (the National Bank of Indonesia) and became a member of the Provisional People's Council, a kind of transitory legislative assembly for the new republic.

Sumitro, meanwhile, obtained his PhD in economics in Rotterdam and took up a series of cabinet positions in trade, economics and finance in the fragile governments of the early post-independence period. Sumitro was a member of the Socialist Party of Indonesia who distilled his thinking in a concept he called "economic democracy", which sought to address structural economic challenges through redistribution. But Sumitro's political ascent was cut short when, dogged by rumours of party corruption and cronyism, and publicly eviscerated as a "foreign stooge" for capitalism, he fled cabinet for a rival republic on the island of Sumatra, known as the Revolutionary Government of the Republic of Indonesia (PRRI). The fall of the PRRI in 1958 sent Sumitro into self-imposed exile, first in Singapore, then in Malaysia, Hong Kong, France, Switzerland and the United Kingdom, along with his family, including Margono; his Christian wife, Dora; two elder daughters, Maryani and Bianti; baby son, Hashim; and five-year-old Prabowo Subianto.

Prabowo has reflected publicly many times on this period of familial isolation. At the dinner table, Margono would recount the heroism of his two dead sons, Sujono and Subianto, whose name Prabowo bears. Subianto and Sujono had been part of a group of rash young activists who kidnapped the future president Sukarno to hasten the declaration of Indonesia's independence. Both later died in 1946, in a battle known as the Lengkong incident, during the Japanese occupation. Prabowo credits these accounts with instilling in him a deep desire for military service and a sense of the great significance of the Djojohadikusumos for the course of Indonesia. Sumitro, too, often reflected on the party conflicts that roiled the early days of the republic and on his momentous decision to lump in with the doomed PRRI movement. Perhaps some inkling of those dinner-table conversations was captured in Sumitro's later writings:

> [H]istory doesn't forgive those who miss an opportunity of historic moment … Those who are too impetuous … and are eager to force history may get a second chance if they survive, but never those who miss their historic moments.

Prabowo also likes to remind his foreign audiences that, as a child in Singapore and Hong Kong, then still under British rule, brown-skinned boys like him had limited access to public spaces. "We know how demeaning it is to be considered second, third, fourth class," he has emphasised. This dissonance must have been vexing for a young Prabowo, whose class status nonetheless secured him entry into the elite schools of the very globalists against whom he would later rail in campaign speeches: the Victoria Institution in Kuala Lumpur, the Glenealy Junior School in Hong Kong, the Zurich International School for high school and the American School in London, from which he graduated in 1968.

By then, of course, a bloody and authoritarian regime called the "New Order" was emerging in Indonesia after two years of mass killings of supposed "leftists", orchestrated and executed by General Suharto and the Indonesian military and supported by Western allies. Facing a country economically in tatters, now purged of its artists, writers, thinkers, scientists and scholars, President Suharto called Dr Sumitro back home.

As Sumitro took up the reins as trade minister, Prabowo entered the military academy (AKABRI) in Magelang in 1970 but graduated a year later than his cohort, in 1974, after being held back for disciplinary reasons. Prabowo also stood out because, at the time, enrolling in the Indonesian military was the fallback option for the sons of Indonesia's poor, not its erudite bluebloods. These were determinative years for the New Order's military, the Armed Forces of the Republic of Indonesia (ABRI), which produced key generals such as future president Susilo Bambang Yudhoyono and future ABRI head Wiranto. More importantly, these graduating years vastly dwarfed any future cohort, producing a crop of ambitious soldiers whose fight for the spoils of power would spark intra-elite competition that would shape the course of Indonesian political history.

Like many of the authoritarian militaries of this period, ABRI was the dominant coercive institution of the regime: it expected to govern, and to reap profits. Its expanded role in political and economic life was known as "*dwi-fungsi*", or dual function. ABRI held a quarter of the seats in the national and regional parliaments, as well as in the People's

Consultative Assembly (MPR), which under the New Order appointed the president in five-year terms. "Greenshirts" (the name whispered on the streets) were spread throughout the New Order administration, as ministers in cabinet, directors-general of the bureaucracy, ambassadors and provincial governors.

A key plank in ABRI's power was, and continues to be, its territorial structure, also known as the KODAM structure (or "Military Regional Commands"), which slices the country into fifteen regions and essentially places a military command of corresponding size at every tier of regional government, right down to the village level. It is a structure that snubs territorial borders to face inwards, guarding the regime against treachery and oppositional forces. This structure reflected ABRI's true purpose, to maintain internal security and defend the New Order from dissent. But this structure also led to unparalleled economic clout, creating opportunities for military businesses to dominate the extraction of natural resources and for generals to open up joint ventures with aspiring economic magnates. In this way, Indonesia's emerging bourgeoise was deeply intertwined with military power.

A young ambitious general, then as now, would expect a slow series of rotations and promotions circulating around this territorial command, currying political and private-sector support, before finally obtaining their first gold star as a general. As the outsized graduating cohorts of 1968 to 1970 coursed through the command, plump positions became increasingly contested, with shorter tenure times marked by rapacious extraction while in post.

Prabowo, by contrast, was one of the few to build his career in the military special forces, known as Kopassus, specialising in covert operations, insurgency, intelligence and psychological warfare. Prabowo joined Kopassus (then known as Kopassandha) upon graduation, a year before Indonesia's annexation of Timor-Leste. Timor would go on to shape much of his career, honing his counterinsurgency skills and building him a loyal power base that has followed him all the way to the presidential palace.

Made in Timor

In 1983, Falintil, the armed wing of the resistance movement, orchestrated "*levantemento*", a bloody collapse of the 1983 ceasefire triggered by the massacre of eighteen ABRI soldiers by Timorese auxiliaries to the platoon. *Chega!*, the Commission for Reception, Truth and Reconciliation in East Timor's account of the occupation, documents how Kopassandha, and in particular the Chandraca 8 Anti-Terror unit, jointly established by Prabowo and the current minister for maritime affairs, General Luhut Panjaitan, was instrumental in managing the fallout, killing and disappearing of over 530 people, including two bloody massacres of dozens of women and children surrendering on the slopes of Mount Bibileo. Chandraca 8 also kept civilians imprisoned in a concentration camp at Kalerek Mutin, in Kraras, where four or five people died of hunger each day.

By 1993, as ABRI sought new methods to defeat the Timorese resistance, Kopassus had become the "central pillar" of the military occupation. Now married to President Suharto's daughter Siti Hediati

Haryadi (known as "Titiek"), Prabowo was back in Java, heading the Kopassus III training centre in Batujajar, West Java, which Douglas Kammen of the National University of Singapore has called "the nerve centre for Timor operations". Here, Prabowo, who had graduated at the top of the class from US military anti-terror training in Fort Bragg (1980), West Germany (1981) and Fort Benning (1985), schooled soldiers in propaganda, terror, kidnapping and sabotage.

Throughout the 1990s, Prabowo, and by default Kopassus, was the lynchpin of the US–Indonesia military relationship, able to connect the US armed forces to other areas of ABRI, and indeed to the inner Suharto circle. To the United States and other allies, Prabowo was an especially valued contact given the large-scale personnel changes in the Indonesian military command as the military tried to accommodate its bloated upper echelons.

But Prabowo was a field man through and through. As Kammen has observed, "for Prabowo East Timor was like home". Timor was Prabowo's laboratory for managing political insurgency, producing techniques that were replicated in bloody operations that targeted civilian populations in Aceh and West Papua. He would be spotted on the streets of Dili, having simply "turned up" without command knowledge or approval. He learned to cultivate and mobilise civilian militia, who would not only provide surveillance on the ground but could disorder and terrorise popular movements.

Among his many young protégés was Eurico Guterres, whom he plucked out to run the Garda Paksi, or Youth Guard for Integration, ostensibly a youth employment agency but that really provided the military with intelligence and captured local criminal rackets. Guterres was ultimately indicted by the UN Special Panels for Serious Crimes for crimes against humanity as head of the Aitarak pro-integration militia group in the wake of Timor's vote for independence.

Prabowo's strategy of cultivating ultra-nationalists, criminal gangs, hardline anti–ethnic Chinese Islamist militia groups and, most incredibly, his own former human rights victims as a spoiler against wider political movements are a motif of his career, repeated in the melee of 1998, in his 2014 and 2019 presidential campaigns, and through the "202 movement" in 2017–18 to agitate against the Jokowi government.

Another tactic Prabowo sharpened in Timor was the orchestration of crises to destabilise rivals and consolidate his grasp on power. Scholars have long argued that Prabowo had a hand in the 1991 Santa Cruz massacre, where at least 250 Timorese were murdered after Indonesian soldiers inexplicably opened fire before an international audience. Factional rivals were purged soon after. Similarly, in July 1996, as head of Kopassus, Prabowo and his coterie, including Sjafrie Sjamsuddin, Zacky Makarim and Muchdi Purwopranjono, were accused of involvement in the takeover of a "free speech forum" run by Megawati Sukarnoputri's opposition party PDI, sparking a two-day mass riot. In the fallout, the Prabowo faction was able to depose rivals from top military posts, capture key military positions and initiate a restructuring of Kopassus, providing Prabowo with his second military star. Flanked by his wife, Titiek – who herself ruled over an empire of toll roads, sat in cabinet and served as deputy chairperson of the regime's political party, Golkar – Prabowo seemed destined to be anointed successor to the ageing President Suharto.

But then came the 1997 Asian financial crisis, which hit Indonesia hard. Within six months, the rupiah was worth 30 per cent of its previous value. As the economic crisis churned into a social and political revolution, Prabowo allegedly amplified the anti-regime unrest fomenting on the streets by instigating anti-Chinese riots along the north coast of central and east Java, and later in the heart of the capital to disgrace his rival General Wiranto, the head of the military. In Jakarta, as waves of protest roiled the capital, Prabowo formed a Kopassus crack team known as *Tim Mawar* ("Rose Team"), which kidnapped dozens of student demonstrators in three waves from the streets. Prabowo and Rose Team took responsibility for the second group of abductions, who were tortured but eventually released. The young people disappeared in the first and third waves have never reappeared.

On 12 May, as the city reached boiling point, four students at Trisakti University were shot and killed by unknown security forces stationed on a flyover road. The deaths remain shrouded in mystery. Not only were the students engaged in peaceful campus protest, but Trisakti University was a private tertiary institution attended by Jakarta's rich kids, who were latecomers to the wider reform movement. Prabowo continues to deny allegations that his men were responsible.

Nonetheless, the Trisakti killings sent the crisis into freefall. In the days leading up to Suharto's resignation on 21 May, many assumed that the Indonesian military would step in to reassume power, but the years of backlogged promotions and rotations had fragmented ABRI's upper echelons and soured them on prolonging the New Order. Into the breach stepped a Prabowo ally, Vice President B.J. Habibie, who assumed the presidency.

This was Prabowo's moment to "force history". That same day, according to Habibie's autobiography, Prabowo demanded he promote the Army Chief, General Subagyo Hadisiswowo, to Commander in Chief of ABRI, and Prabowo himself to Army Chief of Staff. Instead, Habibie snubbed the Prabowo faction by handing the top job to his archrival Wiranto. Infuriated, Prabowo led a party of Kopassus loyalists to Habibie's home, but Habibie got wind of his plans and was quickly airlifted to the presidential palace for safety. After being hauled before a military honour board to testify on the student abductions in August 1998, Prabowo was forced to retire. Soon after, he went into exile in Jordan at the invitation of an old Fort Benning chum, King Abdullah II. Other ports of call, such as the United States, barred the former general from entry, as Prabowo discovered in 2000 when he tried to attend his son's graduation. (The US lifted its ban in 2020 after Prabowo was made defence minister in the Jokowi cabinet.) Australia and the United Kingdom, which do not formally retain blacklists, also quietly dissuaded any visa applications. (Australia reportedly allowed visits by Prabowo from 2014.)

The family rises

For many in Indonesia, these facts of Prabowo's history are old news, recapped so many times that they have lost their political punch. Indeed, few political careers are as well documented as his. Yet how Indonesia's next president amassed close to A$200 million in personal wealth has never been clear. In 2000, Prabowo purchased Kiani Kertas, a pulp and paper company accused of illegal logging formerly owned by Suharto crony Bob Hasan, rebranding it Nusantara Energy shortly after returning to Indonesia in 2001. Today, through Nusantara Corp, co-owned with younger brother Hashim, Prabowo has investments in pulp and paper, forestry, agriculture, mining and commercial fishing, all sectors targeted by his incoming government's big push for energy and food sufficiency.

Indeed, much of the Djojohadikusomo fortune has been generated by Hashim, the family tycoon, who used Prabowo's regime connections to extend the family's economic empire. In the mid-1990s, Hashim and his sister-in-law Titiek were the Indonesian partners in the Paiton 1 project, a massive coal-fired power complex in East Java that *The Wall Street Journal* described as "one of the most expensive power deals of the decade, anywhere"; it sought to charge the state electricity company a mark-up of between 30 and 40 per cent. In this way, Hashim is, as Australian scholars Edward Aspinall and Marcus Mietzner have written, "a product of the Suharto regime's ability to transform the members of leading bureaucratic families into apex capitalists".

In the wake of the Asian financial crisis, Hashim pursued investments in the Middle East and North Asia while living in one of the family villas in Geneva, now repossessed in lieu of over US$158 million in unpaid taxes to the Swiss government. In 2006, Hashim cashed out his share in Kazak oil assets to China International Trust for a whopping US$1.9 billion, some of which he spent on his brother's presidential campaigns. Like Nusantara Energy, Hashim's Arsari Group deals in Indonesian natural resource extraction and processing – palm oil, rubber, tin, pulp and paper, bioethanol, agribusiness – and is worth nearly a billion US dollars. He has invested heavily in scholarly efforts to rehabilitate the legacy of the Djojohadikusumo name by supporting historical research and films about the family legacy. Oh, and funding a Sumatran tiger sanctuary, the acquisition *du jour* of Indonesia's moguls.

But Hashim is not just the family's financier. He is also the architect of its pivot to electoral politics. The party that Prabowo ostensibly leads, Gerindra, or the Greater Indonesia Party, was supposedly Hashim's idea. The party's origin story is wild – a brainwave hatched in the back of a cab between Hashim, then on trial for stealing Javanese artefacts, and the inflammatory former Islamic student activist Fadli Zon (another of Prabowo's Kopassus-era cultivations). Railing with indignation, together they agreed, according to the party's website, that "democracy had been hijacked by irresponsible actors with large amounts of capital. The result being that the *rakyat* (little people) just become a tool [of their interests]. In fact, anyone who doesn't have political and economic power can become a victim to them ... and one such victim was Hashim himself."

Absent from this origin story is Gerindra's historical roots in Parindra (the Greater Indonesia Party), a little-known political party established in 1936 by Prabowo and Hashim's grandfather Margono and a group of conservative Indonesian nationalist societies including Budi Utomo. While other nationalist parties were shaped by more radical ideological visions of social democracy or Marxism, Parinda was the intellectual product of "the Leiden School", a cohort of organicist legal scholars who believed that Indonesian culture was essentially harmonious and consensual and that these traditions should be echoed in the country's political and legal institutions. Although support for Parindra eventually collapsed – the party never quite lived down its reputation for re-enacting Nazi ceremonials – the ideological currents of organicism were key to the resilience of Suharto's particular brand of authoritarian rule. Organicism was the rationale behind the New Order's highly centralised and militarised machinery, its compression of civil society into a few state-chartered corporatist bodies, its sacralisation of the state ideology of Pancasila, the regime's pathological obsession with romanticised representations of Javanese village life, and its self-projection as a "family state" over which the benevolent patriarch Suharto would always preside.

Prabowo and Hashim founded Gerindra, like Parindra, with a small cohort of Islamists, capitalists and military generals, including long-time Kopassus loyalists Syafrie and Muchdie (the latter somehow emerged unscathed from a 2008 trial in which he was accused of ordering the murder of the human rights activist Munir Said Thalib, who was poisoned on a flight to Amsterdam in 2004). In its early years, the party was credited for attracting bright young talent whose political aspirations had been curtailed by Indonesia's cartel party system.

Following the 2014 elections, the party has become more solidly a family affair. While Hashim's son Aryo has given up his parliamentary seat to return to Arsari Group, Hashim's daughter Saraswati, her husband, Harwendro, and a nephew of Hashim and Prabowo, Budi Djiwandono (the child of their sister Bianti), are all elected members in the national parliament. Harwendro and Budi are members in seats in which the Djojohadikusumos have natural resource interests. In addition, Harwendro has secured the role of deputy chair of the powerful legislative commission that overseas agriculture, environment, forestry and maritime affairs. The other son of Bianti, Thomas Djiwandono, is Gerindra's treasurer and a member of the tiny fistful of six Gerindra confidents who make up the Prabowo transition taskforce (renamed the "synchronisation team" in a nod to President Jokowi's indispensable patronage). In July 2024, Thomas was promoted by Jokowi to Second Deputy Minister of Finance. We are likely to see more of the Djojohadikusumo clan take up chairs in Prabowo's new cabinet.

We might well shrug Gerindra off as just another vehicle for Indonesian dynasty, like Megawati Sukarnoputri's Democratic Party of Struggle (PDIP) or Susilo Bambang Yudhoyono's Democratic Party, but Gerindra's manifesto is more than the usual blur of religious-nationalist guff. It argues for a return to the original 1945 Indonesian constitution as a necessary "correction" to the democratic reforms of the *Reformasi* movement, which have generated "national political instability" and slowed economic development. What Indonesia needs, reckons Gerindra, is a purification of the current economic and political system to reflect the "identity and soul" of Indonesia. That is, the democratic principles of contestation, opposition and dissent are replaced with traditional Javanese customs of "harmony" and "consensus-based decision-making". Thus, the pledge to reimplement an "original presidential system of government" is about winding back direct presidential and regional head elections in favour of a centralised system in which the People's Consultative Assembly appoints the president, the president appoints his lackeys in the provinces, a handful of parties demarcate the boundaries of political contestation, and Indonesia's brave and effervescent civil society is whittled down to few state-sanctioned representatives of Pancasila diversity.

The comeback

For many, Prabowo's election as president marks the resurrection of New Order authoritarianism by a forgetful young electorate. For others, it is another manifestation of the Trumpian right-wing populism currently sweeping the globe. Both arguments are mistaken. Voter turnout rates in Indonesia are reliably above 80 per cent at the national level and around 70 per cent for regional elections. Frankly, Indonesians relish the opportunity to pick their governments and to kick them out. For all the evidence of dirty money and candidate vote-buying, Indonesians still regard policy platforms and performance in government as the main basis for their voting preferences. This is a country that loves its democracy and its freedoms, despite the system's many flaws.

Having failed to win a popular mandate for a more "pure implementation of the presidential system" in 2014 and 2019, Prabowo has stepped up again to force history through a strategy of elite negotiation. He and his coalition seized on Jokowi's craven ambitions for his family and legacy, and his tempestuous relationship with his nominating party, Megawati's PDIP, to court the outgoing president. Indeed, Prabowo himself was rumoured to have first dangled the prospect of the vice presidency to Jokowi's firstborn, Gibran Rakabuming Raka. During the campaign, Prabowo shed his nationalist safari suits, the horses in dressage and Mussolini cosplay of his 2014 and 2019 campaigns for work shirts that mirrored Jokowi's presidential uniform. The roaring, hyper-masculine speeches lambasting the elite forces that would destroy the country were gone. Instead, his answers on policy were distinctly beta male, asserting continuity and taking care to reassure the electorate that the president's prized white elephant, the construction of the new capital, would continue.

While Gerindra shut down questions about its manifesto, the Indonesian public were presented with a chubby avatar cushioned from the prickly questions of journalists by a gaggle of YouTube and TikTok influencers pushing the cuddly uncle as their presidential pick. Jokowi used his presidential powers to pork-barrel in key constituencies, annexed legal and judicial institutions to harass and disable rival coalitions, and deployed police to twist the arm of potential dissenters and sources of opposition. The effect was a decisive win to the Prabowo/Gibran pairing, with 58 per cent in the first round, though Gerindra's contest for the house only yielded a middling 13 per cent of seats.

Having been gifted a nascent authoritarian state architecture by the outgoing president, Prabowo and his political allies will seek to institutionalise a model of Indonesian state organicism. Prabowo's strategy is to seek a new deal among Indonesia's elites, in which they will govern through an expansive coalition that will, as far as politically possible, consolidate their power and limit the scope of political competition and dissent. This is the reason Prabowo opens every speech with long and elaborate salutations to every dignitary in the room. This is what the former general means when he reminds his audiences again and again that the failure or success of a civilisation hinges on the unity of its elite classes. While power will be exercised through a fistful of loyalists in cabinet, Prabowo seeks a regime that will nonetheless be underpinned by an outsized governing coalition satiated by the grubby politics of *bagi-bagi* (divvying up the spoils).

The carrot in this strategy is the reassertion of the state as a mechanism for natural resource extraction and as a distributor of market share for the elites. This is what Prabowo gestures to with his big policy platform of national energy and food self-sufficiency, packaged within the infeasible populism of free school lunches. Prabowo's model of food security envisions the conversion of millions of hectares of forested land – "over 12 million hectares of degraded rainforest", as Hashim is wont to repeat – into vast, monolithic plantations. It doesn't really matter that, so far, his involvement in the proposal to build food estates across some 800,000 hectares of forest and peatland in North Sumatra, Central Kalimantan and Papua through the defence ministry has ended in failure. Prabowo is, in essence, proposing a colossal land grab, from which plantation permits, supply chains and food and energy processing monopolies will be doled out to a waiting brood of domestic conglomerates, tech billionaires, ex-military and intelligence tsars, resource-hungry oligarchs, dynasties and party apparatchiks. Seen in this light, Prabowo's regular exhortations for "food and energy sovereignty" are a clarion call to Indonesia's elites to regroup around a new political economy of natural wealth extraction, one in which every elite interest is invested, everyone gets their bit and – most importantly – everyone knows their place.

On the stump, Prabowo's voice cracks with woe when he describes how his free lunch program will relieve the grinding hunger of Indonesia's "little people", reiterating his dedication to ameliorate the suffering of ordinary Indonesians. So far, so *noblesse oblige*. Elsewhere, Prabowo has offered up uncanny accounts of people dying of starvation by his tent on the mountain slopes of Timor, presumably in the concentration camps he established and ran, as the emotional fodder for his food security program.

There are many problems with this strategy, but the main one is that there's not much in it for the kind of country Indonesia has become.

Poverty rates have dropped from 40 per cent to 20 per cent of the population since the early 2000s. Extreme poverty in Indonesia is certainly a problem, but it now stands at 10 per cent. Indonesia's economic and social policymaking now needs to reckon with the rise of an enormous class of "working non-poor", who aspire to social mobility but are trapped in cycles of financial precarity and insecurity. Indeed, Prabowo's most loyal voting base come from this very stratum: the youths educated at high school and university who are deeply frustrated by the gap between the promises of development and the low-paid, low-skilled jobs that Jokowi's middle-income Indonesia could provide.

Indonesia is not, and indeed never has been, the docile population of peasants of Prabowo's imagining. Over the past twenty-five years of *Reformasi*, Indonesia has become a deeply unequal, digital-savvy, highly urbanised, geographically mobile and politically organised middle-income country in need of an economic and industrial strategy that can generate sustained employment with a more egalitarian distribution of wealth, life and opportunity. This is the policy golden goose that would require a massive deconstruction of the very political and economic system that has elevated the Djojohadikusumos to power.

Prabowo's feudal representations of his populace need to be seen for what they are: a pre-game strategy through which dissenters and oppositional figures can be attacked as foreign stooges or anti-government meddlers, unrepresentative of the "true" moral majority, whose aspirations should be as modest as their social status. What happens when Indonesia's people express rights instead of gratitude?

We should expect that Prabowo, a blueblood who has for decades fermented in his own briny destiny, will not shy from forcing history once again.

Democracy and the future

What does this mean for us? Why should Australia's foreign-policy thinkers and decision-makers care about the prospect of a further descent towards authoritarianism under President Prabowo? Certainly, our administration didn't so much as flicker as the coalition aligned with Jokowi harassed Indonesia's journalists, civil rights activists and academics with junk defamation cases. Over the two terms of Jokowi's presidency, we have been untroubled by his government's silencing and displacement of Indonesia's reformers and professionals and activists on the Constitutional Court, on the Audit Board, at the Judicial Commission, at the General Elections Commission and at Indonesia's prized Corruption Eradication Commission. We have witnessed Indonesia's civil space being whittled thin. After all, as Department of Foreign Affairs and Trade staffers have asked me, what has Indonesia's declining civil and political rights record got to do with Australia's trade and foreign policy?

The short answer is that these political dynamics have grave consequences for Indonesia's ability to provide the predictability, rule of law and due process necessary to Australia, Indonesia and our common prosperity. Australia has done much to build and support cohorts of professionals and bureaucrats committed to bringing about good governance and a more equitable rule of law through technical support and by opening up opportunities for mutual learning and exchange. This is important work, but in itself it is not enough.

A response to Indonesia's democracy trouble must lie in our clear-eyed recognition that, with this election, ordinary Indonesians have not voted for the organicist manifesto that the Prabowo camp will now agitate to install. Indonesians, in fact, cherish their democracy and have no intention of surrendering it to oligarchy. Since *Reformasi,* Australia has largely equated supporting Indonesian democracy with helping Indonesians to build institutions or produce "good" policies. Twenty-six years on from Indonesia's democratic transition, plainly this was wrong. Democracy is not merely a technical matter, sealed up in "good" institutions. Rather, the health of a democracy should be measured in the space it permits for popular participation and contestation. In every democracy, that space must be pried open and defended anew – by writers, journalists, workers, artists, activists, bureaucrats, economists, unionists, small-scale landholders, farmers, fishermen, environmentalists, lawyers, teachers, accountants, doctors, scientists and scholars. In Indonesia, these groups have long been on the back foot, especially during the consolidation of the national elite under the Jokowi presidency.

Australia's shift from "development aid" to a broader platform of engagement and partnership with Indonesia means we are well placed to help sustain these groups, by providing opportunities that value and advance their work. We should ward against anything so instrumentalist as "policy reform". Instead, we can support these groups by connecting them to each other and to Australian partners through fellowships, residencies and study exchanges, and by providing the platforms to elevate and promote high-quality work. We need to provide these vital social groups with avenues of respite from regime pressure, as well as create paths for them to further their standing. For Australia, supporting Indonesian democracy means rethinking our often managerialist and risk-averse engagement with Indonesia, so that we better support these groups to exercise fundamental norms, including collective organising and action, scientific expertise, academic and journalistic freedom, artistic licence, bureaucratic independence, and other ethical and professional standards.

As nations, we have been here before. Beneath a sometimes fickle political and economic relationship, Australia and Indonesia share an informal history, often forgotten, in which ordinary people forged genuine networks of camaraderie across a shared geography. The Australian government likes to refer to this as "people-to-people" relations, but the phrase diminishes the richness of the relations of care, curiosity and solidarity that have bonded our nations. Unions, universities, media outlets, galleries and civil society organisations have provided shelter and sustenance to Indonesia's cause during their struggle for independence, after the bloody killings of 1965 and, most notably, during the long, dark years of the New Order. To confront Indonesia's political future, it is to this shared history that we must return. ■

THE ILLUSIONIST

Exposing the Modi cult

Priya Chacko

A few years ago, I attended a public lecture by a visiting official of India's ruling Bharatiya Janata Party (BJP). The official had the audience – mostly members of Australia's growing Indian diaspora – in raptures as he rattled off what he claimed were the many achievements of the Indian government under Narendra Modi's leadership. During the question-and-answer session, I pointed out that the official didn't discuss job creation and private investment, and asked why both were stagnating under Modi. The official laughed and conceded that private investment was a concern, but said India's employment data was flawed. This is now a standard response from the Modi regime to questions about jobs. Later, he approached me with a big grin. "I was really scared of the questions you were going to ask," he said, "because you know the truth!"

After he was unceremoniously dumped as BJP leader in favour of Modi in 2013, L.K. Advani, whose "Hindutva" politics of resentment against Muslims and secular "elites" drove the party's rise in Indian politics, tartly refused to describe Modi as his "protégé". Modi, he said, was a "brilliant event manager". Indeed, crafting and managing illusions has been the hallmark of Modi's prime ministership.

Modi has worked hard to craft the illusion of himself as a *vikas purush*, or "development man", surrounded by an aura of popular benign dominance. His image has been plastered everywhere from billboards and bus stands to COVID-19 vaccination certificates. His personas include kindly uncle, guru, priest, hardworking common man, generous provider, inspirational leader and international statesman.

During the 2024 election campaign, Modi's personality cult reached new heights. He told interviewers he had "non-biological" origins and was an emissary of *Parmatma* (God), who "keeps making me do things". In January, he consecrated a temple to the god Ram, becoming a quasi-religious figure. The Ram temple was hastily built in time for the election, on the ruins of a sixteenth-century mosque. This followed a decades-old campaign by Hindutva activists, led by Advani and assisted by Modi, then a party worker, to reclaim the site from Muslims. The campaign culminated in the destruction of the mosque in 1992 and a spate of violence across northern and western India, resulting in the deaths of more than 2000 people, mostly Muslims. The Supreme Court accepted Hindu claims to the site in 2019. Built as a symbol of the new India, the temple was meant to pave Modi's way to winning a record 400 seats out of the 543 seats in the lower house of the Indian parliament.

The election confirmed India's transformation into an electoral autocracy with an unlevel playing field. An opaque electoral financing system, the Electoral Bonds Scheme, has made the BJP by far India's richest political party. The opposition Congress Party's accounts were frozen before the campaign for alleged tax violations. Two opposition chief ministers, Arvind Kejriwal and Hemant Soren, were jailed on weak charges of corruption. Independent media organisations faced tax investigations and censorship. The Election Commission of India declined to investigate multiple reports of candidate and voter intimidation, or to assess concerns about electronic voting machines.

But elections are dangerous times for the rulers of electoral autocracies. While public dissent can have dire consequences, the ballot box gives everyone a voice. A pre-election survey conducted by the Centre for the Study of Developing Societies revealed high levels of discontent over unemployment and inflation. Interviews conducted by independent journalists and researchers revealed that voters were angry about the government's withholding of resources from state governments; they were concerned that the BJP might change the Constitution to remove affirmative action for lower castes; they disapproved of its arrests of opponents; and they worried about the threat of dictatorship. Voters were also unhappy with the BJP's strategy of encouraging and coercing defections from other parties. This practice, known as the BJP's "washing machine", irked party workers, who were reluctant to mobilise votes for candidates they did not like.

Despite local and international media predictions, and the uneven electoral playing field, the 2024 election was a blow for Modi, whose party lost its parliamentary majority. Modi won his own seat of Varanasi, a major Hindu pilgrimage site, but his margin dropped by a third.

Yet the result is unlikely to chasten Modi, and while he is in power Indian democracy remains in peril. He has already started to craft and manage illusions to explain his setback and to justify his unrelenting grip on power, relying on the ideological tropes and political tactics that he has been deploying throughout his career.

Development man

Modi was once seen as too extreme to be a national leader. In 2005, as Chief Minister of Gujarat, he was denied a visa to travel to the United States due to his alleged failure to prevent the deaths of more than 1000 people (mostly Muslim) in communal violence following an accidental train fire which was blamed on Muslims. This violence had serious consequences for Gujarat's already-slowing economy, leading to a decline in investment. Modi worked assiduously to remake himself as a technocrat/chief executive officer, presenting himself as *vikas purush*. With the help of an American public relations firm, APCO Worldwide, which is notorious for its work with autocrats, his "Vibrant Gujarat" investment summit transformed from a small event into "India's Davos", attracting sponsorship from business lobbies in the United States, the United Kingdom and Australia.

Using neoliberal World Bank buzzwords, he spoke of "good governance", "performance accountability" and "peoples' participation", and of using technology to eliminate corruption. He linked these concepts to lessons from ancient Vedic-era texts such as the *Mahabharata* and *Ramayana*. "[T]he concept of Ram Rajya [Ram's holy kingdom] and the advice given by Lord Krishan to Arjuna in *Gita* [the *Bhagavad Gita*] is only about good governance," he claimed in a speech in 2010.

As the anti-caste leader and drafter of the Indian Constitution, B.R. Ambedkar pointed out, the *Mahabharata* and *Ramayana* are concerned with maintaining caste and gender inequalities. The open-endedness of these texts has inspired retellings that challenge the caste norms and patriarchy they uphold, but these were not the versions pursued by Modi in Gujarat.

Hindutva is often described as majoritarianism or religious nationalism, but to appreciate its social impact (which goes beyond instigating religious discord) and its inherently anti-democratic character, it is better understood as a form of organicism. Inspired by European organicist and neo-Vedantic philosophies, the founding fathers of Hindutva, mostly middle-class Brahmins at the top of the caste order, naturalised social hierarchies and inequality. Deendayal Upadhyaya, a leader of the BJP's parent organisation, the Rashtriya Swayamsevak Sangh (RSS), and author of the BJP's guiding doctrine, "integral humanism", conceived the national body as a *virat purusha* (cosmic man) with a Hindu soul (*chitti*) and limbs analogous to the ancient *varna* caste order of Brahmin priests (head), Kshatriya warriors (arms), Vaishya agriculturalists and traders (abdomen) and Shudra workers (legs). In this hierarchy, individuals had differentiated duties to serve the collective, rather than rights or interests.

Modi champions this philosophy of duties over rights. "India lost considerable time because duties were not accorded priority," he said during an event hosted by a controversial Hindu organisation, the Brahma Kumaris, in 2022. "We can make up for the gap which has been created due to primacy about rights while keeping duties at bay in these 75 years by discharging duties in the next 25 years."

In the 1950s and 1960s, Upadhyaya's organicism led to his advocacy of policies favouring the RSS's core supporters in small-scale industries. Modi's organicism centres on "wealth creators" working as a family with managers and workers to produce trickle-down development. This reflects the emergence of upper-caste, upper-middle-class professionals as a part of the BJP's core base in the 1990s.

Hindutva regards social and political division as pathological

Gujarat did rapidly grow due to investments in infrastructure. But its growth rates and levels of private investment were inflated. Modi's Gujarat model was underpinned by debt-fuelled crony capitalism, with a few companies dominating key sectors. Tax cuts, subsidies, incentives and exemptions for business and the rich, urban, upper-caste middle classes led to large deficits and a reliance on indirect taxation.

Spending on health and education was kept low and services were privatised. Gujarati companies were favoured. The result was high levels of inequality, middling human development and the rise of Gujarati oligarchs, including Gautam Adani and brothers Mukesh and Anil Ambani.

Hindutva regards social and political division as pathological. In Gujarat, power was centralised and personalised. The judiciary and police were politicised, and the state parliament was marginalised. Extrajudicial killings of Muslims were justified as preventing terrorism. Hindutva vigilante groups undertook moral policing and critics of the government were targeted with surveillance. Modi accused non-government organisations (NGOs) critical of government policies of being self-serving, anti-national and obstructionist. *The Right to Information Act*, he claimed, was being used by vested interests to harass the government.

All of this was obscured with publicity campaigns trumpeting business success stories and photoshoots of Modi in Western business attire. Once dubbed the "Butcher of Gujarat", by 2011 he was being hailed by the financial press as a "benignly tyrannical CEO". Content with their handouts, incentives and concessions, industrialists such as Ratan Tata extolled Modi's vision and pleasant persona.

The Modi regime

After Modi was elected prime minister in 2014, the United States dropped its visa ban and Barack Obama penned an article in *Time* magazine calling him the "reformer-in-chief".

Modi scaled up his Gujarat model to the national level, with similar outcomes. India's economy has grown, driven by debt-fuelled infrastructure spending and consumption. Gujarati oligarchs became national oligarchs. Adani, the industrialist closest to Modi, scored contracts in sectors in which his company had no experience, and benefited from the privatisation of ports and airports.

Private investment and jobs, however, continue to stagnate. The "Make in India" and "Atmanirbhar Bharat" ("Self-Reliant India") schemes, involving production subsidies and other incentives, have failed to produce a manufacturing sector that is able to provide mass employment.

Policies like the sudden COVID lockdown and agricultural reforms were introduced with little consultation with stakeholders, government departments or parliament. Farmers continue to protest, and small businesses continue to suffer. India has experienced a K-shaped pandemic recovery, with spikes in luxury consumption but falling consumption in middle- and lower-income households.

As in Gujarat, Modi has accused NGOs of victimising him and funding "anti-national" activities that slow India's economic growth. Tens of thousands of organisations have lost their licences to access foreign funding, ending critical service delivery and costing thousands of jobs. Amendments to *The Right to Information Act* make it increasingly difficult to gain access to public expenditure data or to query inaction against corrupt officials. By 2019 even some industrialists were lamenting the "environment of fear" that deterred them from criticising the government's policies.

Following the Gujarat model, job creation has been low, and inequality has risen. Public-sector employment, a crucial avenue for social mobility, has been shrinking. According to the Centre for Monitoring Indian Economy, an independent think tank, India's unemployment rate rose to 9.2 per cent in June 2024. According to the World Inequality Lab, inequality in India is now higher than it was under the British Raj. In 2022–23, the top 1 per cent of income earners held 40 per cent of the wealth share. Asked about the report, Modi replied, "So should everybody be poor? If everyone is poor, then there will be no difference."

A Citigroup India report argues that India will struggle to create sufficient jobs for its young population, even if a 7 per cent growth rate is sustained over the next decade. The worst affected by unemployment are the most marginalised: Muslims, women, Dalits and Adivasis (tribal peoples).

The Modi regime disputes these statistics or minimises their importance. Accusing the opposition of spreading false narratives, it has cited Reserve Bank of India (RBI) data suggesting employment has increased. However, the RBI defines employment so broadly that it includes unpaid work.

The masses, government officials assert, care only about their living standards, not inequality. While spending on health and education remains low, the government says it has improved living standards through schemes that subsidise the purchase of goods such as toilets and cooking gas and that provide food rations.

Modi has a lower-caste background and portrays himself as a lowly tea-seller who has empowered the poor. He claims to have replaced traditional forms of caste stratification with four new castes of welfare "beneficiaries": women, farmers, the youth and the poor. The provision of subsidies, small loans and cash transfers, delivered via a digital platform that claims to eliminate corruption, are said to trigger "aspirations" among the poor to perform their duties through self-help entrepreneurship. But academic studies have shown that corruption still occurs; poor households are excluded due to technical failures; and cash transfers, loans and food rations ensure only survival, not lifestyle improvements.

Nonetheless, the government says it has pulled 248 million Indians out of poverty. Such claims are difficult to verify. India was once a world leader in collecting economic statistics; since 2014 there has been a precipitous decline in both the availability and quality of its data. The census, last held in 2011, has been indefinitely postponed. The household consumption expenditure survey, which is traditionally used to estimate poverty, was undertaken in 2017–18 but withheld on the basis that it was of poor quality. Leaked data from the survey indicated a fall in consumption among the poor. The director of the institute that produced the National Family Health Survey 5 was suspended when the results were contrary to the government's statements about the reach and effectiveness of its welfare schemes. A World Bank working paper with similar findings was withdrawn after complaints from the government.

The election

Typically, Modi presents himself as a benign and humble leader of the nation. Occasionally, however, he has transformed into a political brawler, again deploying tactics he used in Gujarat. Secular and liberal Indians have been deemed deracinated and self-interested and accused of pandering to religious minorities and promoting foreign ideologies. Critics and opposition parties have been dismissed as corrupt, dynasts, Muslim appeasers and "urban Naxals" (Maoists). University students, journalists and activists have been charged and jailed without trial or bail for offences ranging from sedition to terrorism to attempting to assassinate Modi. Many were also allegedly targeted with Israeli Pegasus spyware. This repression was enabled by strengthening already draconian laws, and by relying on cooperative courts and compliant investigative agencies.

But Modi left the dirtiest work associated with Hindutva to colleagues and vigilante groups. India's Muslim and Christian minorities are regarded as potentially disloyal because their holy lands are outside India. Humiliating Muslims, India's poorest religious minority, is central to Hindutva politics. Muslims, as co-religionists of the historical Moghul rulers, are characterised as enslavers of Hindus. Modi's right-hand man, home affairs minister Amit Shah, often describes Bangladeshi immigrants as infiltrators and termites, and has boasted of his party's ability to spread fake news. The Chief Minister of Uttar Pradesh, Yogi Adityanath, a priest who has his own militia, bulldozes the homes of Muslims who protest the government's policies or are accused of crimes. He and other BJP chief ministers have introduced or strengthened policies that target Muslims. Laws curtailing beef consumption, interreligious marriage and religious conversion are enforced by police and vigilante groups, which monitor, harass and lynch those suspected of transgressions.

To maintain a façade of benign and successful leadership, Modi has tried to stay clear of bad news stories, leaving problems to fester. He stayed silent for months when hundreds of thousands of farmers protested in 2020 and 2021 against his government's agricultural policies. When he spoke, it was to claim that his government was the victim of a foreign conspiracy by professional protestors. While Modi eventually withdrew the policies, the farmers' grievances remain unaddressed. He is yet to visit the BJP-ruled state of Manipur, where conflict between the Meiti and Kuki communities has resulted in more than 200 deaths and the displacement of more than 60,000 people.

Campaigns matter in Indian elections. By the middle of his campaign in 2024, Modi was clearly worried. While in March he was extolling his welfare schemes and the Ram temple, by April he had moved to rousing anti-Muslim sentiment. In a string of speeches in Maharashtra, Rajasthan, Uttar Pradesh and West Bengal, Modi claimed the opposition would snatch Hindus' land, property, buffalos, affirmative action rights and wedding jewellery to give to Muslims. Invoking conspiracy theories about Muslim population growth (akin to the "Great Replacement" conspiracies of the Western far right), he spoke of Muslims as "those who have large numbers of children" and as "infiltrators". At one point he even accused the Congress of taking money from Adani and Ambani.

Exit polls predicted a sweeping victory for Modi, but pollsters admitted that their sampling was affected by the reluctance of poor, lower-caste voters in Uttar Pradesh, Maharashtra and West Bengal to reveal their true voting intentions for fear of violence from electoral workers.

This part of the electorate punished the BJP, which lost one-third of its rural seats, including in the states most active in the 2020–21 farmers' protests. It also lost one-third of its seats which are reserved for Dalit candidates. Modi's anti-Muslim speeches failed to stem the BJP's losses – the party lost twenty of the twenty-two constituencies in which he made those speeches. For the first time in a decade, the BJP's parliamentary majority depends on the support of its National Democratic Alliance (NDA) partners, particularly the fickle and ambitious chief ministers of Bihar and Andhra Pradesh, the Janata Dal's Nitish Kumar and the Telugu Desam Party's N. Chandrababu Naidu.

Regional dynamics proved crucial. The Congress Party almost doubled its seat share, making gains in Rajasthan, Haryana and Maharashtra among rural voters and particular regional castes. The BJP and the NDA made gains or consolidated where regional party opposition was weak (as in Madhya Pradesh and Gujarat) or faced high levels of anti-incumbency (as in Odisha).

The election burst the twin illusions of Modi's unassailable popularity and of the haplessness of the opposition. In West Bengal, Chief Minister Mamata Banerjee of the All India Trinamool Congress won big with the female voters Modi was targeting. Female candidates won 38 per cent of her party's seats, three times that of the BJP.

In the crucial state of Uttar Pradesh, the Deakin University–educated former chief minister Akhilesh Yadav won back lower-caste voters from the BJP by preselecting a broader range of lower-caste candidates for his Samajwadi Party. His campaign emphasised unity to save the Constitution. Modi spent much of the campaign trying to combat the claim that the BJP intended to abolish lower-caste affirmative action, but the party's antipathy for the policy was well known.

Rahul Gandhi's baggage of dynastic elitism has been exploited in the past by Modi, who refers to the Congress Party leader as "*shehzada*" ("prince") and "*pappu*" ("dim-witted boy"). But in the past two years Gandhi has undergone a transformation, seeking to cultivate an image as a man of the people. In 2022–23, he undertook a five-month-long, 4000-kilometre Bharat Jodo Yatra ("Unite India March") across the country, drawing large crowds, to protest the government's communal politics and authoritarianism. His conviction for defamation (later overturned), for claiming that many with the surname "Modi" have been found to be corrupt, added to his street cred. Prior to the election he undertook a two-month Nyay Yatra ("Justice March"), to draw attention to unemployment, inflation, inequality and caste, anticipating key election issues. He was often in the company of Mallikarjun Kharge, a veteran Dalit leader who succeeded Sonia Gandhi as Congress Party president in 2022.

The election result was not a complete rejection of Hindutva

Gandhi's "*yatra*" politics has continued after the election. He has visited camps for the displaced in Manipur, railway workers in Delhi and cobblers in Sultanpur. As the rest of the political class arrived in Mumbai in July for the US$100-million wedding of the Ambani scion to rub shoulders with Kim Kardashian and Tony Blair, Gandhi was spotted having dinner in a Delhi pizzeria. With Akhilesh Yadav, he has launched strident attacks in parliament on the BJP's crony capitalism and resistance to a socioeconomic caste census. Caste is likely to be a defining issue of Modi's third term, with the potential to bring down the government. His NDA ally Nitish Kumar has already conducted a caste census in his state of Bihar.

The election result was not a complete rejection of Hindutva. Fringe Hindutva preoccupations – such as the bogey of Muslim appeasement and the Ram temple – have become normalised, particularly in northern India. Rahul Gandhi avoids directly advocating for Muslims, instead promoting inclusion. In electoral contests, however, Hindutva had its limits. Embarrassingly, the BJP lost the seat of Ayodhya, where the Ram temple was built. "We are pleased about the [Ram] temple," said one Ayodhya resident displaced by the temple, "but we are grieving inside. Those were our life savings. We are persecuted because we are poor. Ramji [the god Ram] did not say that the poor must be kicked out." To add insult to injury, the chief priest of the Ram temple announced that it is now leaking due to heavy rains and poor construction.

The world's friend

The BJP's 2024 election manifesto fashioned India as *vishwa bandhu* ("world's friend"). "We have established Bharat [India] as a reliable, trusted and dependable voice globally in the last ten years," it asserted. The government has worked hard to create the impression that Modi is a prominent and trustworthy global player. A much-satirised BJP election advertisement featured a young woman meeting her father at an Indian airport exclaiming, "*War rukwa di papa!*" ("He stopped the war, Father!"), suggesting that Modi negotiated a ceasefire in Ukraine to allow trapped students to leave. The Ministry of External Affairs later had to deny the claim.

This image of global prominence played to middle-class Indians' craving for international respect and exploited Western desires for an "un-China", as *Time*'s international editor deemed India in 2006. A pre-election survey found that India's international image was the third-most liked achievement of the Modi government. Global leaders continued to celebrate India as the world's largest democracy, even as it was downgraded on various democracy indices. To counter this, the government portrayed India as the "mother of democracy" at the 2023 G20 summit. A booklet distributed to delegates did not trace the origins of Indian democracy to its modern Constitution, which enshrines fundamental rights, but to ancient texts and kingdoms such as the Chola Empire. The prevalence of gender- and caste-based domestic servitude and slavery in the Chola period was, of course, not mentioned.

Modi's autocratic turn was unfortunate for his Western democratic friends but bearable. His refusal to condemn Russia's invasion of Ukraine was accepted on the grounds of India's historical reliance on Russian weapons and its energy needs. The United States exempted India from economic sanctions after it purchased the Russian S-400 missile defence system, and looked away when Indian public oil companies bought stakes in Russian oilfields. Modi succeeded in softening the optics by urging Putin to end the war while expressing concerns about casualties.

India's military weakness against China underlies its recent outreach to the United States and its greater enthusiasm for the Quad. In January, Defence Secretary Giridhar Aramane admitted that US support was crucial during India's border clash with China in 2020, which remains a stalemate. "[We] are standing against a bully in a very determined fashion," Aramane said at a defence collaboration meeting earlier this year; "we expect that our friend, the US, will be there with us in case we need their support." But the expectation that India will reciprocate is an illusion. Questioned about India's reactive approach to China along the border, the external affairs minister, Subramanyam Jaishankar, responded: "They are the bigger economy – what I am going to do? I am a smaller economy. Am I going to sort of pick up a fight with a bigger economy?"

In 2020, following the border clash, the government introduced tariffs, non-tariff barriers and production incentives to grow local industry and curb reliance on Chinese investment, services and products. These policies have largely failed. While India has attracted some global investment for mobile phone assembly, this remains dependent on importing Chinese components and machinery. In 2023, Chinese imports reached record levels, making it India's top trading partner. Business groups and government ministries have been lobbying for a loosening of trade, investment and visa restrictions. Chinese manufacturers are already involved in Apple smartphone assembly in India. Some import duties have been relaxed for mobile phone components, and the government has indicated it will approve visas for Chinese technicians. Adani has been permitted to use cranes manufactured by the Chinese state-owned company ZPMC, which was accused in March 2024 of espionage in a US congressional probe, for its mega-port in Kerala.

At the same time, the Modi government fears Russia's and China's deepening alliance, which has spurred its tighter embrace of Russia. India has become the largest buyer of Russian crude oil, which accounts for more than 40 per cent of its oil imports. This energy dependence looks set to deepen, facilitated by alternative payment systems designed to skirt Western sanctions. While India's weapons purchases are decreasing, its economic constraints may limit its ability to move towards more expensive Western weapons. Joint manufacturing in India may sustain its Russian arsenal.

The Modi regime's alignment with Russia does not end at importing cheap oil, weapons and hugs with Putin. It increasingly shares repressive values with Russia and other autocratic states. Russia was a pioneer in using laws to restrict the operations of civil society groups, something the Modi regime has become adept at. They now work in concert with an unofficial "Like-Minded Group" of states, including China and Iran, in the NGO Committee of the United Nations Economic and Social Council to vote against human rights NGO applications for consultative status.

India is also a member of Interpol's Executive Committee, and in 2022 voted against an attempt to have Russia suspended from access to Interpol databases. Russia has been a prolific user of Interpol red notices (arrest alerts) against dissidents residing abroad. India too has been accused of abusing Interpol red and blue notices (requests for information) to try to return those it accuses of being terrorists.

Foreign interference

The Modi regime is alleged to have used various tools of transnational repression against diaspora activists, journalists and academics. These measures include visa cancellations, surveillance, intimidation and threatening family members in India. These tactics result in self-censorship among the Indian diaspora and violate the sovereignty of states with diaspora populations.

Numerous incidents have been reported by diaspora members in Germany, Sweden, the United States, the United Kingdom, New Zealand and Australia. The Indian government threatens and punishes diaspora members by revoking their Overseas Citizenship of India cards, which confer travel and permanent residency rights. OCI cards have been cancelled for "defaming India", tarnishing "the image of the country" and creating "biased negative perception".

In 2023, India was accused by the Canadian and American governments of plotting assassinations of their citizens who are supporters of the Sikh separatist movement in India. Indian officials have refuted these accusations, blaming rogue agents for the botched assassination of Gurpatwant Singh Pannun in the United States, and denying the successful Canadian assassination of Hardeep Singh Nijjar. But Modi leaned into this new reputation during the election campaign. "[T]his new India enters the house and kills," he proclaimed at a rally in Charu, Rajasthan. In 2024, India was also accused of interfering in Canadian elections, including by providing financial support to pro-India candidates through proxy agents.

India faced a violent separatist movement agitating for an independent Sikh state of Khalistan in the 1980s. This culminated in the army raiding the Golden Temple, Sikhism's holiest shrine, to capture militants, and the subsequent assassination of Indira Gandhi by her Sikh bodyguards, followed by anti-Sikh violence, with complicity of Congress leaders, which led to 3000 deaths. Through a mixture of repression and exhaustion the movement gradually dissipated, but some Sikhs who live abroad continue to advocate for the cause, and the Indian authorities have continued to pursue them. While support for the movement in India remains scant, the Modi government's desire to delegitimise protesting farmers (many of whom were Sikh) by linking them to foreign Sikh separatists, along with the security establishment's eagerness to use more aggressive tactics, has made it a potent international issue.

Like Russia, India under Modi has become a key source of global disinformation and digital authoritarianism targeting diaspora dissidents and critics. India has blocked the websites of dissident diaspora groups, used internet shutdowns to quell dissent, issued social media takedown orders against critics and blocked critical YouTube content by Indian and foreign media, including Australia's ABC and Juice Media.

Pro-Hindutva social media accounts, which view Israel as an inspiration and ally, spread an extensive anti-Palestinian disinformation campaign at the beginning of the Israel–Hamas War. This was amplified by BJP officials and government ministers. Social media accounts have also spread disinformation about the prevalence of attacks on Hindus in the violence that followed the downfall of Bangladesh's government, reinforcing the key BJP narrative of "*Hindu khatre mein*" ("Hindus are in danger"). This disinformation circulates in pro-government diaspora WhatsApp groups, including in Australia, fuelling Islamophobia. BJP leaders have also circulated the posts of an organisation called the Disinfo Lab, which is allegedly run by an Indian intelligence officer. The Disinfo Lab releases personal information about diaspora critics and crafts elaborate conspiracies linking them and Indian opposition leaders with Pakistan, Islamists and the global far right's favourite object of hate, George Soros.

The Hindutva movement has long been influenced by the global far right; its founders drew inspiration from Nazism and Italian fascism and its current leaders utilise contemporary tropes. The BJP's social media campaigns have depicted Rahul Gandhi as a puppet of

Soros, while Hindutva leaders Mohan Bhagwat and Ram Madhav have denounced "cultural Marxism" for bringing chaos to India. The BJP's youth wing, the Bharatiya Janata Yuva Morcha, participated in a conference in February 2024 with the Heritage Foundation's Kevin Roberts to discuss topics such as "wokeism". Roberts is the founder of Project 2025, which aims to institutionalise ultraconservative policies and concentrate power in the executive under a Trump administration.

Beyond illusions

India has long been a flawed democracy. Some features of Modi's government, such as the centralisation of power, repression of minorities and dissidents, crony capitalism and deepening economic inequality, have been evident in state and national governments led by other parties. However, the Modi government's inherently authoritarian organicist politics of Hindutva has entrenched these illiberal and anti-democratic traits.

The new Modi cabinet contains most of the same faces and includes no Muslims. Soon after the election it was business as usual. The government approved the prosecution of the writer Arundhati Roy and Kashmiri legal scholar Sheikh Showkat Hussain under anti-terrorism laws for speeches they gave fourteen years ago at an event on Kashmiri independence. Amit Shah has made numerous anti-Muslim speeches, as has Yogi Adityanath, who blamed a foreign conspiracy for the BJP's loss in Uttar Pradesh. The BJP government of Madhya Pradesh demolished the homes of Muslims accused of possessing beef. The BJP-ruled states of Madhya Pradesh, Uttar Pradesh and Uttarakhand passed an order (later stayed by the Supreme Court) making it mandatory for restaurants along a Hindu pilgrimage route to display the names of the owners and staff, a move intended to target Muslims. A leaked draft of a proposed Broadcasting Bill included measures to rein in independent online content creators in India and abroad who provided alternative news commentary to the pro-government mainstream media during the 2024 election.

The post-election budget in July was lacklustre, containing few promising initiatives for India's masses of unemployed and angering even the pro-government media for its tax hikes for the middle class. Given the pressure from voters to create jobs, a quiet expansion of Chinese trade and investment appears imminent.

Modi's first post-election international visit was to Russia, where he enthusiastically hugged Putin, describing him as a "dear friend". This prompted public castigation from Volodymyr Zelenskyy and warnings from the US ambassador to India, Eric Garcetti, that the US–India relationship is "not yet deep enough" to be taken for granted. The Indian government's response was curt. "In a multipolar world, all countries have the freedom of choice," said its foreign affairs spokesperson, Randhir Jaiswal. Modi's subsequent visit to Ukraine resulted in an awkward hug with Zelenskyy, but little changed in India's position.

Australian leaders have wrapped themselves in the Modi illusion in the hope of ingratiating themselves to an India that might serve as a strategic and economic bulwark against China. The Department of

Foreign Affairs and Trade's India country reports continue to classify Muslims as being at low risk of discrimination, probably to deter asylum claims from Indians, which have grown rapidly in the past decade. Reports of the Modi regime's monitoring of diaspora critics by a "nest of spies" in Australia, which has long been suspected in the community, only surfaced when information was leaked to *The Washington Post*. Australian politicians continue to repeat the tired slogan that India is the world's largest democracy with shared values and interests. This approach does little for Australian sovereignty or security, or for its credentials as a country committed to democracy and a rules-based order because it allows India to evade accountability. Introducing measures to deter transnational repression, such as publicly naming all perpetrators and their activities and criminalising and prosecuting the monitoring of diaspora dissidents (as in Sweden and Germany) would be steps in the right direction.

Dealing with an increasingly autocratic India will be a critical challenge for Australia

Anyone expecting a more conciliatory Narendra Modi following his loss of a parliamentary majority will have been sorely disappointed by his first speech as a third-term prime minister. In a two-hour speech filled with half-truths and mistruths, Modi, who has a penchant for speaking of himself in the third person, beat his chest to declare that "Modi is still strong". All criticisms of his government were labelled the "anti-national conspiracies" of an "eco-system" determined to "derail India's progress". "Today," he said, "I want to tell the eco-system that its every conspiracy will now be answered in its own language. Today," he went on, "India attacks by entering homes."

Dealing with an increasingly autocratic India, which represses internally and externally while aligning with like-minded countries to reshape international institutions in illiberal directions, will be a critical challenge for Australia during Modi's third term. The outcomes of other countries' more confrontational approaches suggest the costs are manageable. Since 2014, German courts have convicted five Indian intelligence assets for spying on Sikh, Kashmiri and Tamil dissidents, with little impact on Germany–India relations. India has been muted in response to the US prosecution of an Indian national for attempted assassination. While the premature revelation of Canada's assassination charges against India (prompted by the leaking of the investigation to the media) has seen their diplomatic relations nosedive, the Canada–India trade relationship has grown since the allegations came to light. Australia should not jeopardise its sovereignty and the international rules-based order by perpetuating the Modi illusion through silence and pandering. ■

THE FIX

Solving Australia's foreign affairs challenges

Connor O'Brien on Why Australia Should Support an Ambitious Global Tax on Maritime Emissions

"If Australia wants to partner with the Pacific on climate action, it needs to support redistributive global tax measures that combat carbon emissions while also addressing ballooning climate finance needs."

THE PROBLEM: Growth in seaborne trade, which constitutes over 80 per cent of international trade in goods, has led to rising greenhouse-gas emissions. International ships, particularly bulk carriers, oil tankers and container ships, contribute approximately 2.9 per cent to global emissions. While fuel efficiency standards have improved, they have not kept pace with overall shipping growth. In fact, global shipping remains stubbornly difficult to decarbonise due to a lack of investment in developing alternative fuels, green shipping assets and infrastructure.

While some jurisdictions, such as the European Union, plan to increase taxes on aviation emissions, maritime emissions are largely untaxed due to the cross-border nature of international shipping. International Maritime Organization (IMO) members have committed to reducing the carbon intensity of international shipping by 40 per cent by 2030, before reaching net zero by 2050. However, member states are yet to agree on the measures required to realise these targets.

As a leading fossil-fuel exporter, Australia has a moral and political obligation to combat maritime emissions. However, unlike the United States and China, Australia is too small to unilaterally remake the global green transition through its own policymaking. Its constrained development assistance budget cannot meet existing needs in the Pacific region, let alone across all climate-vulnerable states.

This predicament calls for robust climate multilateralism. Australia needs to reinvigorate its climate diplomacy, lest it be left to face the consequences of unilateral subsidies and tariffs that disadvantage it economically – or, worse, fail to act at all.

THE PROPOSAL: Australia should back a global tax on maritime emissions. In particular, Australia should endorse a proposal by Belize and the Pacific island countries (PICs) for a minimum US$150 per tonne universal levy on maritime greenhouse-gas emissions.

Negotiations regarding a levy on maritime emissions are already well progressed within the IMO. At a meeting in March 2024, member states committed to endorsing an emissions pricing mechanism by April 2025. However, the ambition of existing proposals varies significantly. Thirty-four countries currently support a universal mandatory levy on maritime emissions in some form. Most ambitiously, Belize and a coalition of PICs support a levy of a minimum US$150 per tonne from 2027. Such a levy could generate US$80 billion in revenue annually. This amount would nearly surpass all existing climate finance flows from developed states, which only recently achieved – albeit belatedly – their annual US$100 billion target.

But a coalition led by China opposes a universal levy. It has instead proposed an International Maritime Sustainable Fuels and Fund mechanism. Importantly, the China-led coalition supports the less ambitious "tank-to-wake" measure of fuel consumption, which excludes "well-to-tank" emissions. Under this complex proposal, ships would first be required to meet target fuel-intensity measures. These targets would be linked to the sustainability of each fuel type, from dirty fuels such as methanol and natural gas to clean fuels such as bio-methanol and green hydrogen. Ships that exceed their targets would be awarded surplus credits, which they could choose to sell to under-compliant ships, bank for future years or cash in for compensation from a sustainable shipping fund. The dollar value of the surplus credits would be set at a sufficiently high level to incentivise underperforming shipping companies to lower their emissions.

Between these two positions, various alternatives have been put forward. The European proposal combines a fuel-intensity mechanism with a complementary levy. It also adopts the more comprehensive "well-to-wake" measure of emissions. Alternatively, Japan's "feebate" proposal would require a mandatory financial contribution on all "tank-to-wake" emissions, which would be used to fund rebates for ships that adopt eligible green fuels.

So far, Australia has not put its name to a specific proposal, but reportedly sided with the China-led coalition at an IMO committee meeting in July 2023 and opposed a Marshall Islands and Solomon Islands–led proposal for an emissions levy of US$100 per tonne. At the time, federal transport minister Catherine King stated that Australia, as an island nation dependent on imports and exports by sea, needed to carefully consider each proposal. However, Australia's leading maritime industry body, Shipping Australia, has previously expressed support for an IMO-backed and globally coordinated maritime emissions levy.

To formulate its approach, the Albanese government recently conducted a round of public consultations on a Maritime Emissions Reduction National Action Plan, which will outline a pathway for reducing shipping emissions. This process provides the government with a unique opportunity to build consensus in support of an ambitious global tax on maritime emissions. It could announce its support for the Belize and PICs–led proposal in advance of the April 2025 meeting of the IMO's Maritime Environment Protection Committee, at which the emissions pricing mechanism will be decided.

WHY IT WILL WORK: Australia is an IMO foundation member. It also holds a seat on the IMO Council, as one of the ten states with the largest interest in international seaborne trade. If Australia threw its weight behind Belize and the PICs, it would significantly ramp up pressure on the China-led coalition to accept a compromise deal.

An ambitious universal levy would assist global efforts to facilitate a just green transition in several important ways. The multi-billion-dollar revenues could be used to fast-track the development of zero-emissions fuels, enable technological transfer to low-income states and even compensate for environmental loss and damage. These revenues would go some way towards addressing the dramatic shortage of funds to address climate needs in low-income countries, especially small island states.

A universal levy would also provide the clearest and least administratively onerous pricing signal to shipping companies. This would reduce existing uncertainty regarding future costs, which is driven by speculation about the form of a future global shipping tax. It would also encourage shipping companies to accelerate their decarbonisation plans to reduce their future tax burden. They could do so by investing in and adopting green fuels, as well as technological innovations such as harnessing ocean currents to reduce fuel consumption. While significant, the cost of the levy would be lower than fuel price volatility, meaning that it would not excessively hamper global shipping trade.

Importantly, the Belize and PICs proposal would place the burden of financing maritime decarbonisation on shipping companies, rather than on taxpayers. This is particularly attractive for Australia, where taxes on fossil fuels are manifestly inadequate, and public appetite for spending more on overseas climate finance is low. Ambitious action on maritime emissions would also boost Australia's nascent green hydrogen industry, given green hydrogen's importance to global maritime decarbonisation plans. Such action could therefore play a central role in helping Australia to realise its ambition of becoming a renewable energy superpower.

If implemented, a maritime emissions levy would create a critical precedent showing that global taxes can work, both diplomatically and logistically. Australia could then advocate for similar levies on aviation emissions and the fossil-fuel trade. These measures would generate even greater revenues for PICs to finance climate adaptation and mitigation, while deterring global emissions.

Supporting PICs on this issue would be a major diplomatic win for Australia. It would signal that Australia is willing to defend the collective interests of the region in multilateral forums, even if doing so might at times conflict with its direct self-interest. If Australia wants to partner with the Pacific on climate action, it needs to support redistributive global tax measures that combat carbon emissions while also addressing ballooning climate finance needs. Until Australia begins making these kinds of decisions consistently, its commitment to Pacific regionalism will lack credibility.

Finally, an ambitious maritime emissions levy would provide a critical building block for Australia's proposal to co-host, with PICs, the United Nations Climate Change Conference of the Parties 31 (COP31) in 2026. Co-hosting this event would not only decrease unease in the region regarding Australia's lack of climate action, but also provide a capstone policy to announce in the lead-up to the summit. For Australia's proposed COP31 summit to be a success, it would need to coordinate and deliver these sorts of breakthroughs consistently. Otherwise, hosting the conference would only further entrench Australia's negative global reputation on climate change. ■

Reviews

Nuked: The Submarine Fiasco that Sank Australia's Sovereignty
Andrew Fowler
Melbourne University Press

In the growing body of informed analysis of the AUKUS trilateral agreement, even supporters of the broad thrust of the policy have expressed alarm about the secrecy surrounding its development and the political manipulation that accompanied its endorsement. Others have canvassed more profound reservations about the foreign policy implications of the agreement, especially for Australia's sovereignty and our relationships with our near neighbours. More than a few have asked why this shift was necessary at all, and whether the core element – the purchase and construction of nuclear-powered submarines – is in Australia's best interests, or even achievable. Serious doubts have also been expressed about the projected costs, delivery schedules and nuclear waste management protocols.

One recent contribution is from investigative journalist Andrew Fowler, who, in *Nuked: The Submarine Fiasco that Sank Australia's Sovereignty*, forensically examines the dynamics of the decision, the major players – largely hidden and unknown to most Australians – and the risks attached to a tightening alliance with an increasingly unstable and unpredictable United States.

The problem with analyses such as this is that they come after the fact: the Coalition and Labor parties had committed to AUKUS before any independent, informed investigation and public debate were possible. Moreover, both are now apparently unwilling to entertain any doubts about a deal that has already cost Australia $850 million (to pay off the French boatbuilders whose contract was cancelled) and an unknown amount – perhaps as much as $4 billion – already incurred in abandoning the conventional submarine program, which, unlike AUKUS, was embarked on after appropriate due diligence. A further $9.4 billion has been committed to support submarine construction in the United States and the United Kingdom, part of the anticipated total cost of $368 billion.

Fowler's analysis, like others, reveals not only that the AUKUS agreement was developed in great secrecy, but also that it sidelined significant, potentially contrary views within government, was sponsored by a small coterie of enthusiasts for a tighter alliance with the US, deliberately misled the French government and was explicitly designed by the Coalition to "wedge" Labor in the lead-up to a federal election. Any reluctance to endorse the proposal would have been portrayed as evidence that Labor could not be trusted with Australia's national security. Fowler's evidence of behind-the-scenes manoeuvring to undermine the French agreement by players with conflicted interests (including a significant number of US former military personnel) deserves exposure and further investigation.

Secrecy such as this always risks compromising the quality of policymaking and problem analysis: too few voices are heard, alternative viewpoints are excluded and basic assumptions underpinning the policy go unchallenged. In the case of AUKUS, questions that were ignored include projections for long-term US stability and regional influence; whether closer integration with the US might lead to a loss of Australian strategic control; whether the deal complies with the nuclear non-proliferation agreements to which Australia is a signatory; the nature of the risks posed by China's rise; Australia's capacity to deliver the technical expertise required by the program; and the likelihood that the technology might be superseded. When policy development is restricted to those who are strong advocates for a particular solution, questions such as these and alterative courses of action are more likely to be overlooked, the risks minimised and the benefits exaggerated.

What is clear is that the conventional and expected processes of security policy development and defence equipment acquisition were not followed. This is especially troubling given that AUKUS has been described as "a decades-long strategy to deliver the most costly defence project in Australia's history", with profound implications for Australia's defence and security. The way it was developed represents a wholesale abandonment of conventional policymaking processes; most notably, citizens were kept in the dark. The risk this poses to the people's trust in government and willingness to accept its decisions is obvious, and very dangerous in a climate where political trust and engagement are already at alarmingly low levels. Occasions where secrecy in policy development is justified are rare. And the AUKUS decision was not one of them. Paul Keating was not alone in observing that there was "no White Paper, no major ministerial or Prime Ministerial statement to explain to the Australian people what exactly is the threat we are supposedly facing and why nuclear submarines costing more than any project since Federation were the best way to respond to such a threat".

As he and others imply, in a democracy like ours, any formulation of a public policy should begin by asking, "What is the nature of the problem? Is it significant enough to warrant action? And is it amenable to a deliberate policy response?" At the outset, it should be possible to specify the desired outcomes, examining which policies are likely to be the most effective, why it is expected they will be, and on what evidence. It means investigating the details of what is proposed (including realistic costing), whether there might be unanticipated consequences, and the overall balance of benefits and risks. It is prudent to also ask where the policy options originated, being alert to special pleading, rent-seeking and biased, untested advice.

Ideally, the best policy options should be exposed to public view for scrutiny and challenge ahead of their adoption. Secrecy is anathema to democracy, a governing system which depends, for its legitimacy – its social licence – on the informed consent of the governed and on accountable institutions. The free flow of information is needed to ensure that those exercising power are subject to checks both within and outside government: from public servants, independent courts, an independent press, and civil society. Informed, quality public debate is only possible when the information coming to and from government is not distorted by manipulation, strategising and deception, or by restrictions on allowable communication. The genesis and subsequent development of the AUKUS agreement fails on all these grounds.

A dramatic shift in Australia's defence and foreign policy was engineered without Australians' knowledge or consultation, let alone consent. What's more, Labor's dramatic and – given the enforced 24-hour deadline for deliberation – poorly considered decision to endorse the agreement meant there was no serious political contest and the issue was not widely debated ahead of the 2022 election. Nor was its profound significance described frankly to the Australian people. Once elected, Labor did not pause to take public stock of the risks and benefits of the agreement. Indeed, most of the public justification has focused on the potential for local job creation, not the likelihood that the AUKUS agreement "binds decisively Australia to the United States and Great Britain for generations", as a US press briefing asserted. Nor have Australian governments of either stripe taken citizens into their confidence about why the agreement was necessary; how we should resolve the contradiction between our stated self-reliance and the fact that AUKUS ties Australia more firmly than ever to the US warfighting posture; and why we are so conspicuously signing up to a US project aimed at "containing" China, and thus risking engagement in a war over Taiwan.

From Labor there is only silence on why it abandoned its long-held opposition to nuclear power, as well as its previous aspirations for a more independent Australian foreign policy. Surely we can do better than what looks like timid subservience to a declining power.

Carmen Lawrence

The Odd Couple: The Australia–America Relationship
Allan Behm
Upswell Publishing

Bilateral relationships often lend themselves to marital comparisons. Are the countries long-term partners, working together and committed to the same goals? Is one needier than the other? Are they in or out of sync? Bonding? Squabbling?

That kind of human framing, while treacly when applied to geopolitics, can sometimes be illuminating. And in the final chapter of Allan Behm's new book calling for a more mature bond between the United States and Australia, there are some sharp insights to be drawn from his imagining the two countries in couples therapy.

Putting Washington and Canberra on the couch, Behm, a former longtime Australian public servant, zeroes in on what neither country's people and leaders want to talk about: the insecurities that shape behaviour, undermine trust and hold the bond back from where both countries need to go in our fraught, unsettled era. In his view, both nations are in a bit of a rut.

"America," he writes, "long accustomed to acting with a jaunty disregard for international opinion, seems now to experience a kind of decision paralysis as it searches for self-affirmation in its own deeply divided society. And Australia," he adds, "so afraid of putting a foot wrong that it cannot summon up the courage to put a foot right."

In sharper terms, America, the injured alpha, is in deep trouble, struggling with a crisis of confidence, rumination and disagreement over its international role. And so Australia must do more to keep the pair strong. Instead of acquiescing as an acolyte, or "talking big but walking small", Australia needs to grow beyond its insecurities. It needs to speak truth to American power and become a more consequential partner.

Simply put, he concludes: "The management of Australia's most important international relationship must be reimagined and re-engineered."

How? What would Australia leverage, from resources to institutions and culture? What would a re-engineered relationship really look like?

A deep dive into all of that – a book with a strong argument about how Australia might accomplish the task of updating its self-image to go along with its pragmatic policies and sizable gross domestic product – would certainly be welcome. It could be just the tonic that both Washington and Canberra need to rethink what they can do and learn together.

But this is not that book. Everything I've just quoted is in the final few dozen pages. Near the end, there are also a handful of smart ideas: calls for greater investment in diplomacy by Australia, and for a broadening of high-level meetings beyond defence and elitist, private get-togethers like the Australian American Leadership Dialogue.

Unfortunately, these ideas are not fully developed, nor are they as ambitious as they could be. Behm, who spent thirty years in public service, including as an adviser to Penny Wong when she was the shadow minister for foreign affairs, often seems to fall into the same dynamic he identifies in the ranks from which he came: a hesitancy to be bolder and to build a focused case for more innovative foreign policy.

The book is a bit like a fifty-minute therapy session that features a few minutes of memorable insight at the beginning and end, with a whole lot of backstory and grievances in between. Much of the middle offers a tour of American ills, with occasional glances back at Australia. There are a few sections on shameful similarities – such as the entrenched racism and policies of erasure for both countries' Indigenous inhabitants – and a grab bag of bilateral observations.

In a chapter on culture, Behm excoriates the baby boomer generation for being entitled, "grasping solipsists", and then reminisces about the 1950s and '60s, when Americans and Australians read more of the same kinds of mostly American books. It's not exactly clear how or why these observations go together.

Behm's approach is stronger when he draws attention to the two elements of American foreign policy that Washington insiders too often overlook as shapers of international public opinion: the deeply rooted economic protectionism of the United States, which reaches back far beyond Trumpism, undermining faith in the US commitment to equitable trade; and America's tendency across centuries to make war and military intervention the favoured tool of foreign influence.

Several chapters roam widely through World War I and II, exploring America's hesitancy to get involved and ultimate ambivalence towards President Woodrow Wilson's dreams of systemic peace. All of that is then followed by discussion of America's costly foreign adventures – Vietnam, Iraq and so on.

The author's feelings about American power often toggle between attraction and revulsion. He admires Wilson's idealism, seen in his effort to build the League of Nations. He writes that America "is good at working with its partners", citing the collective response to the global financial crisis as an important example. But he returns again and again to what he calls America's "warfare DNA", which in his eyes makes the US a permanent pugilist that has never met a war it didn't want to fight. He never fully reconciles the America of Wilson and the America of Trump.

No country is a monolith, of course, and neither are our opinions, so perhaps Behm's back and forth is its own form of personal therapy. Who among us is not trying to work out how to feel about a frantic, violent, confounding, creative, rich, divided and sometimes inspiring America? But Behm does have a few priors he might wish to reconsider, and other insights that would have benefited from deeper exploration.

He demonises America's military-industrial complex, for example, in a way that feels outdated and exaggerates its power. While the United States still has the world's largest military, the truth is, as many studies have shown, America's defence industrial capacity has been severely diminished since the end of the Cold War. That's part of the reason the United States is pushing Australia to produce more munitions that can be sold to the Pentagon and American partners in the region.

Scepticism generally about the growing defence ties between the

United States and Australia clearly animates Behm, with AUKUS and its nuclear-propelled submarines at the front of his critique. The amount of money spent on a few very complicated tools of war ($400 billion or so) strikes him as an outrageous investment that would have been better spent on other ways to improve the relationship.

That may be true, but when I talk to American and Australian officials, they mostly discuss AUKUS as the catalyst for a re-engineered relationship, not unlike what Behm seems to want. It's really a technology partnership above all else, with benefits and risks that come with making the tools of war a form of bilateral glue.

What the US–Australia relationship now offers is an opportunity for Australia to say and do more – to speak more forcefully to the United States about not just what it does in the world, but also why partnerships among democracies still matter.

There is little sign of this happening anytime soon. When Prime Minister Anthony Albanese was asked, after the assassination attempt on Donald Trump, if he was concerned about political turbulence in America, he demurred and focused on Australia's rash of leadership changes, running down his own country rather than speaking up for its democratic strengths.

It was a classic sign of the insecurities that Behm identifies: Australia insisting it's just a small country with nothing to add. That might have been true in the prime minister's youth, but it is not true anymore – not when Australia has the critical minerals the world needs for an energy transition; not when its location is beyond the reach of Chinese missiles; not when its democracy (despite Canberra's parochial bubble) is among the healthiest and most pragmatic policy generators in the world.

But beyond these obvious areas of strength lies something greater.

Buried in the middle of Behm's interesting missed opportunity of a book is a section that focuses on the rule of law. It's the kind of thing that can often sound boring, as dry and tasteless as breadcrumbs, but Behm quotes a 2017 speech by Foreign Minister Penny Wong that attempts to explain what lies at the root of phrases like the "international rules-based order": human dignity.

Foreign policy for democracies must be steeped, he argues, in the Enlightenment idea that everyone has the right to a life of worth and fulfillment, to chart their own course and pursue happiness.

"Recognition of human dignity and worth provides the energy that drives constructive national and international development policies," Behm writes. "Along with the transformational change that makes the world a better place, it redefines security as a goal that unites rather divides at both the national and international levels."

Maybe the next time Behm or someone else puts Australia and the United States in couples therapy, the discussion can be a bit lighter and more focused on securing dignity at home and abroad. Instead of emphasising insecurities, flaws and resentments, maybe the therapy sessions of the future in Washington and Canberra can focus on the shared values that keep a good relationship going in good times and bad. Call it a reset – or renewal of vows.

Damien Cave

Correspondence

"United front: Australia needs a military alliance with Indonesia" by Sam Roggeveen

Damien Kingsbury

It has been a truism of Australian strategic thinking, dating to before Federation, that the country is vulnerable and requires protection by allies. It is also increasingly apparent that Australia's security, nominally guaranteed by the United States, may be declining just as China becomes the dominant regional power.

It is within this context that the Lowy Institute's Sam Roggeveen has put the proposition that, to secure its strategic interests, Australia should form a military alliance with Indonesia. This idea has, in fact, been floating around Canberra's back corridors since Prime Minister Paul Keating's ill-fated 1995 Australia–Indonesia security pact. After the signing of the 2006 Lombok Treaty, it was reprised by some senior members of the Canberra defence establishment. Now Roggeveen has breathed new life into the notion of an alliance. But there is a tension at the heart of his proposition, between what used to be termed the "Fortress Australia" and "forward defence" strategies.

Roggeveen proposes an "echidna" strategy for Australia, taking a cue from Taiwan's "porcupine" strategy, which is essentially the fortress idea. Yet, as part of that, he proposes an alliance with Indonesia that straddles the equator and that is forward defence. These two approaches have quite different operational methodologies, implying different force posturing and hardware requirements. Roggeveen sidesteps this conundrum by suggesting that the mere existence of an Australia–Indonesia alliance would be sufficient to deter potential challenges. Yet to be a deterrence, the alliance would require substance of a type much greater than he suggests.

There are arguments for such an alliance, the first of which is that it suits Australia to have a buffer between it and an increasingly assertive power. And, should push come to shove, such an alliance would fit the forward defence model of addressing challenges a good distance from Australian shores.

There are, however, also problems with the alliance proposition, the first of which is that it disproportionately benefits Australia. Indonesian strategic thinkers would look at this and ask: "What's in it for us?" Not much, as it transpires; Indonesia has little need for Roggeveen's suggested over-the-horizon radar or upgraded navy when its primary concerns remain internal. Further, despite occasional rhetorical flourishes, there is an almost complete lack of Indonesian elites' trust of Australia. Australia may have signed the 2006 Lombok Treaty, but in Indonesia this is viewed as window dressing. Added to this, and despite minor tensions, Indonesia's approach towards China is much more accommodating than Australia's approach towards China. And, if threatened, Indonesia's defence policy is oriented towards "defence in depth", rather than towards meeting challenges before they arrive.

From Australia's perspective, there is support for a closer strategic relationship with Indonesia, but at various points in the political establishment there is a reciprocal lack of trust. This reflects a view that Indonesia's public commitments might not be backed by its actions: if tested, an alliance could be found wanting.

About fifteen years ago, one senior Australian army officer, floating the Indonesia alliance idea, acknowledged with a chuckle that the Indonesian military were "brutal bastards", something he thought Australia's defence establishment could accept. He acknowledged, however, that Australians more generally might not.

The Lowy Institute's own polling shows that most Australians have a low opinion of Indonesia as a "friend", do not regard it as a functional democracy and believe that its military retains an outsized role in its politics.

Widespread Australian negative perceptions of Indonesia will not be diminished by the next president being Prabowo Subianto, a right-wing nationalist former general and President Suharto's former son-in-law. Prabowo's history of alleged human rights abuses would likely exercise extensive public debate in Australia, should a military alliance start to look like a reality.

Assuming that the United States retreats as a regional partner, and that China extends its assertive posture, the question remains how Australia might enhance its security. Having a well-conceived defensive strategy and equipment and manpower appropriate to its needs is an obvious first step. That, arguably, is in train.

Closer regional relations are also an obvious step. On this, I would suggest a wider rather than a narrower focus, in the first instance building closer training and exercise relations, such as the Indo-Pacific Endeavour. Strategic partnerships are also more regionally palatable than formal alliances.

To achieve this, Australia requires a nuanced understanding of how prospective partners view the evolving strategic environment, and what groundwork might be laid for closer cooperation, should it be requested in changed circumstances. This might not have the same deterrent effect of formal alliances, but partnerships and demonstrated interoperability between Australia and its regional friends would not go unnoticed in Beijing. It is also an approach that would be more welcomed by Australia's regional neighbours.

Damien Kingsbury is emeritus professor at the School of Humanities and Social Sciences, Deakin University, and the author or editor of several books and articles on regional political and security issues.

Robert Law

Sam Roggeveen's argument for pursuing a military alliance with Indonesia is a welcome but ultimately flawed contribution to the debate about Australia's future security in the Indo-Pacific.

While Roggeveen articulates the military logic of such an alliance, he does little to grapple with the political rationale. Military alliances – formal or otherwise – are a manifestation of political will. They stem from close and trusting bilateral ties.

While the relationship is calm on the surface, deep currents underneath are threatening to pull Australia and Indonesia apart. For decades, Indonesia needed Australia more than the reverse. Roggeveen's argument reflects this thinking: an assumption that Indonesia will be in a weaker position if it navigates regional tensions without Australia's support. Such assumptions are becoming outdated as we undergo a historic shift to Australia being the junior partner. By the end of this decade, Indonesia's economy will have overtaken Australia's. There is a heady optimism among Indonesia's political elite, who believe they can chart their own destiny in the region, including dealing with China. Australia has no experience navigating this new landscape.

Against the backdrop of this historic transition, three primary challenges will test the relationship.

The first and most visible is the sharp divergence on managing US–China competition, which Evan Laksmana addresses in his essay. Roggeveen's proposed military alliance holds little appeal for Indonesia, as it has increasing confidence it can navigate regional tensions through non-alignment and a "free and active" foreign policy. While the United States will continue to be an important military partner for training and equipment under a Prabowo administration, Jakarta remains wary of US-led security initiatives. Despite Australia and Indonesia's shared rhetorical commitment to a free and open Indo-Pacific, scratch below the surface and their visions for the region's future diverge sharply.

The second challenge is economic nationalism. Indonesia has always been a half-hearted supporter of the system of free trade established by the Bretton Woods Conference. Its sense of grievance towards the International Monetary Fund after the Asian Financial Crisis only deepened its scepticism. But for a long time it lacked the economic weight for its policies to have a major impact on the international economic system.

This began to change with the adoption of economic nationalist measures under President Susilo Bambang Yudhoyono, and accelerated under President Joko Widodo. The most prominent of these has been the "downstreaming" policies in resources, which banned the export of some raw commodities. The surge in nickel demand due to the renewable energy transition created an opportunity, which Indonesia seized with the help of Chinese investment. Cheap Indonesian nickel has depressed prices and hit Australian miners' profits. Canberra is only now starting to push back by advocating for new green standards for sustainably sourced resources.

Nickel is just the beginning. Prabowo has promised to expand downstreaming beyond resources to agriculture and other sectors. As protectionism grows, Australia and Indonesia will increasingly find themselves at odds, both bilaterally and in global economic forums. This policy divergence is playing out as Australia is pushing for greater trade and investment with Indonesia. The growth prospects are tantalising but business will increasingly be on Jakarta's terms.

The third challenge is democracy. The quality of Indonesia's democracy has declined steadily under Widodo's rule. The once formidable anti-corruption commission has been hobbled and the Constitutional Court co-opted. These were key institutions established after the fall of the Suharto regime to safeguard democracy. Freedom House scored Indonesia 57 out of 100 in 2024, down from 65 in 2017.

When Widodo addressed the Australian parliament in 2020, then Opposition leader Anthony Albanese referred to Indonesia as a blossoming multi-party democracy. Such terminology is increasingly out of place in the bilateral relationship. Indeed, given the historical human rights allegations against Prabowo, it is unlikely that he will be afforded the honour of a parliamentary address in Australia. His track record suggests Indonesian democracy is unlikely to improve under his watch, and could even decline further.

Canberra will need to put more effort into influencing Jakarta's thinking. Moving quickly in a regional crisis will be crucial. A serious Chinese misstep in the South China Sea could provide an opportunity to bolster security ties. Indonesia's interest in joining the Organisation for Economic Co-operation and Development (OECD) opens new avenues for Australia to influence its economic policy. Business has a role to play in supporting high-quality sustainable growth. On the democracy front, we should boost our engagement with the media, civil society, the bureaucracy and the judiciary.

While new differences are coming to the fore, Indonesia and Australia are still bound together by geography. Neither nation has the luxury of opting out. We must find new and creative ways to prevent the deep currents from pulling us further apart.

Robert Law is Director of Advisory & Insights at Asialink Business, and a former diplomat and intelligence analyst.

Melissa Conley Tyler

Between 2011 and 2018 I organised four sessions of the Australia–Indonesia Dialogue, a joint initiative to enhance people-to-people links announced during President Yudhoyono's visit to Australia in 2010. Initially chaired by Australian Institute of International Affairs national president John McCarthy and soon-to-be ambassador Rizal Sukma, it brought together Indonesians and Australians from key sectors to build connections and explore opportunities for closer engagement in business, culture, education, science and technology.

There were moments in which you could see these connections being made. From Opposition, Julie Bishop floated the idea that would become the New Colombo Plan, which has since enabled more than fifty thousand young Australians to study and work in the region. Blackmores CEO Christine Holgate inspired others on the business opportunities of Indonesia's growing middle class. ABC managing director Mark Scott committed to film an episode of *Q&A* in Jakarta. The sultan of Yogyakarta hosted senior Australians at his palace, while New South Wales governor David Hurley welcomed senior Indonesians in Bahasa.

But when I think back, my clearest memory is the shift I saw over the decade: a clear sense of Australia becoming less and less relevant to Indonesia. While we were working hard to get Australia's key sector leaders to see the emerging giant on their doorstep, you could almost see the Indonesians' attention drifting away. I remember one participant putting it starkly after Australia had been headed by five prime ministers in ten years: "You think of us as poor and politically unstable, but isn't it the other way around now?"

I thought of this when reading the important recent edition of Australian Foreign Affairs on the potential for an Australia–Indonesia alliance.

I saw Sam Roggeveen trying to push Australian foreign-policy thinking as far as it can currently go. A military alliance with Indonesia would indeed be Australia's "most ambitious and important foreign-policy initiative of the century so far". He admits that it is far from our present political reality – and would require the next step in our evolution from "Anglo-Saxon outpost" to a "multicultural nation deeply embedded in the economy, security and culture of our neighbourhood".

But, at the moment, this vision simply does not connect with the view of the world from Jakarta, as Evan Laksmana's essay demonstrates. Laksmana says bluntly that Indonesia is unlikely to see Australia as one of the cornerstones of its foreign policy, ranking below ASEAN, the United States, China, Japan, Singapore and Malaysia as priorities. Tellingly, he frames the issue for Jakarta as whether to lean closer to the West. For many Indonesians, that is still how Australia appears: the local branch office of the entity known as "the West".

The problem is that it is difficult to have a strong defence relationship between two countries if this is not underpinned by other ties. The national interest argument may be strong, but if there are not broader affinities, this seed will not take root. Deep relationships require whole-of-nation engagement.

At the government-to-government level, Australia–Indonesia relations are about as good as we could hope. Many of the "beef, boats and Bali" issues that caused ruptures during the last decade have been managed. The gap is elsewhere – in sectors such as business, culture, education and science, where we can see what AFA editor Jonathan Pearlman described in his introduction as "a paucity of understanding or curiosity on both sides". Lowy Institute polling, both in Indonesia and Australia, makes this apparent: both nations show a lack of knowledge about each other and have only moderate levels of trust.

One of the persistent mysteries about the Australia–Indonesia relationship is the difficulty in getting people excited about it. I've been privileged to work alongside some of the true champions who have been grinding away, decade after decade, spruiking the teaching of Asian languages, nurturing Asia literacy and building Asia-capable businesses. But often this feels like a drop in a pond.

During those years I brought together senior Australians and Indonesians, I would find myself imagining that Australia had the sort of relationship with Indonesia that it has with New Zealand. If it did, how much stronger Australia would be.

But until a lot more Australians share this vision, it will not become a reality and the potential will remain unfulfilled. It may be that Australia and Indonesia are "natural strategic partners" – as Professor Tim Lindsey puts it – but they haven't yet learned how to be natural partners.

Roggeveen's proposal for a military alliance will likely fail to attract support, because defence ties alone – no matter how logical or valuable – cannot create the closeness of relationship required. Indonesia will continue to see Australia as a "valuable provider of a specific set of defence needs", as Laksmana describes it, rather than as the type of partner that Roggeveen suggests. For Australia to matter deeply to Indonesia, it needs to engage in the whole range of issues that preoccupy Indonesian leaders, as described by Maria Monica Wihardja: the health, education, skills, social infrastructure, digital economy, green energy transition and other challenges Indonesia needs to surmount to escape the middle-income trap.

For me, this shows the need for those who care about Australia's defence and security to broaden their horizons. Australia's security requires the use of many tools of statecraft, not just defence. National security advocates can be a powerful constituency for whole-of-nation international engagement, which has flow-on security effects. Australia lacks the political will to do something as simple – yet as game-changing – as making Indonesian language a compulsory school subject.

Future historians puzzled by how Australia failed to capitalise on the opportunities of a rising world economy on its border would be well advised to look beyond missed military alliances to a wider relationship that failed to flourish.

Melissa Conley Tyler organised the Australia–Indonesia Dialogue as national executive director of the Australian Institute of International Affairs from 2006 to 2019. She is the executive director of the Asia-Pacific Development, Diplomacy & Defence Dialogue (AP4D).

John Blaxland

Australia's relationship with Indonesia has been a bit like the board game Snakes and Ladders. Incremental progress in the relationship (climbing up the ladder) is easily undone (sliding down the snake) over a range of misunderstandings, including issues such as beef, boats, spies, clemency, Timor and Papua. Both countries have considerable overlapping interests. They have to find a way to deepen the relationship to prevent this cycle from recurring continuously.

In "United Front", Sam Roggeveen proposes an Australia–Indonesia military alliance, on the premise that the two nations "should aim to ensure that China can never dominate them militarily". The call for a hard power alliance is attractive, and builds on their deepening exercises, exchanges and economic cooperation. But it downplays Indonesia's jealously guarded foreign policy independence, and overlooks the benefits that accrue from the Australia–US alliance. Australia needs Indonesia more than vice versa. Mindful of the China challenge, part of the attraction for Indonesia of closer ties with its southern neighbour seems to be that Australia is a US security ally.

Roggeveen's article observes that as the United States has not "responded sufficiently to China's military expansion ... Beijing is betting that the US will eventually give up and go home". This pessimistic view of American priorities overlooks its territorial presence in the Western Pacific and beyond, including the three states with a US compact of free association, Marshall Islands, Micronesia and Palau, not to mention the US sovereign territories of Guam, Hawaii and the Aleutian Islands. To be sure, China wants the United States to retreat from the Western Pacific, but the neighbours disagree, and a simple look at the map shows that America's territorial interests point to an enduring commitment.

The article also claims, without evidence, that Australian nuclear propulsion submarines "will make Australia a military target for China". And this "will force Indonesia into some uncomfortable choices". This assumes Australia was not already a target (the facilities at Pine Gap, Northwest Cape and Tindal likely made the list already) and contradicts the view of most deterrence theorists that weakness invites adventurism. Indonesia itself maintains submarines and has expressed no real qualms about Australia doing so.

The view also overlooks the fact that the proliferation of sophisticated air and space surveillance platforms has eroded the stealth of diesel-electric propulsion submarines – especially over longer distances, where they are required to surface to recharge their batteries ("snorting"). They are also exposed to detection by would-be adversaries supported with near saturation low-earth polar-orbit satellites, along with decades of submarine operations pattern analysis, coupled with AI and airborne weapons (drones, missiles and aircraft). For Australian submarines to transit from Fremantle to any other Australian port requires multiple snorts. Each time, they are exposed to detection, which, during a conflict, would likely prove catastrophic. The only known way around that problem for a country with such a long and exposed coastline is to stay underwater for such transits – and that requires nuclear propulsion.

Roggeveen rightly declares: "Let's not underestimate what Jakarta would be getting: not just a capable partner but a highly reliable one." Yet the model he proposes involves hobbling the Australian military capability options by derailing and disrupting plans for nuclear propulsion submarines and the plans for additional US security engagement in the neighbourhood.

There is scope for the Australia–Indonesia security relationship to deepen further. The Indonesia–Australia Comprehensive Partnership Agreement and the newly inked defence agreement point to the prospect of stronger and closer security and economic ties in future. There is also space for the countries to lead in a "sweet" arrangement, a "MANIS" regional maritime cooperation forum encompassing Malaysia, Australia, New Zealand, Indonesia and Singapore. (The Bahasa word for "sweet" is *manis*.) Other countries, such as Timor-Leste, Thailand, Papua New Guinea and the Philippines, could also be invited to participate. These countries have few opportunities to work together, yet they all share the space at what President Joko Widodo has described as the "maritime fulcrum" of the Indo-Pacific.

This forum could address a range of non-traditional security concerns, and possibly even broker a breakthrough in the Myanmar civil war – in a manner similar to that played by Indonesia, along with Australia and others, in brokering the Cambodian Peace Accord three decades ago. Other topics on which regional representatives could consult are the security implications of climate change, illegal fisheries, natural resources management, illegal immigration, terrorism, smuggling and transnational crime, including trafficking in drugs, endangered wildlife and weapons. The forum could also focus on improving search and rescue and natural disaster coordination. That approach would involve collaborative government, university and think tank teams from the participating countries forming working groups on police, immigration, border security, legal, judicial, environmental, intelligence and financial matters.

Ultimately, this forum could take regional cooperation beyond the levels achieved through the Bali Process and help to address the implications of a new security agenda centred on environmentally vulnerable communities and climate change. Eventually, military and other security concerns could feature as well. For instance, efforts could be made to coordinate regional coast-watching aerial surveillance patrols, exchange information, and establish additional police and other liaison and exchange positions.

Critics might argue that there are too many regional forums already. But existing forums have great difficulty reaching consensus. A smaller grouping like MANIS would find it easier. Potentially, it could bolster regional stability in a way that circumvents the existing consensus-driven constraints.

Despite the ups and downs along the way, Australia and Indonesia are indeed at the fulcrum of the Indo-Pacific. Roggeveen is right to argue that they need to work together more closely. Australians must invest more in learning about Indonesia. Joint initiatives to counter environmental degradation and in response to climate change would help. Indonesia and Australia have a shared destiny and are not natural adversaries. Both countries need to work hard to make that destiny peaceful and prosperous.

John Blaxland is professor of international security and intelligence studies at the Australian National University's Strategic and Defence Studies Centre.

Sam Roggeveen responds

Call me a stubborn optimist, but I'm encouraged by the tenor of the responses to "United Front". Yes, they are all critical, but in a particular way.

If we divide the criticisms into two classes – 1. This is a bad idea in principle; and 2. It is unachievable in practice – then they belong overwhelmingly to the second group. Why is that encouraging? Because it suggests these critics agree that a military alliance between Australia and Indonesia is desirable, even if they think it is so unlikely as to be not worth considering.

I'll come back to the practical roadblocks below, but let's first consider the arguments that this is a bad idea, made by Damien Kingsbury, who claims that such an arrangement could entangle Australia in a conflict with China.

Kingsbury says an alliance would "straddle the equator" and is therefore a form of "forward defence". But the alliance I propose is not in tension with the continental defence model I proposed in *The Echidna Strategy*; rather, it is a natural extension of it. Indonesia and Australia occupy a single strategic space, in which a threat to the vital interests of one is also a threat to the other, so planning to fight together makes sense. I propose a purely defensive arrangement designed to create a "bubble" over the maritime region, such that no adversary can safely operate ships and aircraft within it. It isn't designed to project power but to stop others doing so.

Kingsbury, Robert Law and John Blaxland all make the same observation: Australia needs Indonesia more than the other way around, so what's in this proposal for Indonesia? They have found a weak spot in my argument, because the attractiveness of this deal for Jakarta will diminish as Indonesia grows. Still, for now, Australia's economy remains appreciably larger and our defence force much more capable for the mission I recommend. Australia already has many of the means to create a bubble over maritime South-East Asia, and we can help Indonesia develop similar capabilities much faster than if they try to do it alone. Australia can also offer Indonesia certainty and assurance that it will never again have to think about Australia as a security risk. Even the most suspicious and mistrustful in Jakarta's security establishment, who still fear Australian support for West Papuan independence, can be placated. The US and Canada boast the longest undefended land border in the world; Indonesia and Australia should aspire to have a similar relationship across their maritime border.

Every correspondent describes formidable practical barriers to my proposal. Law summarises them succinctly: "While Roggeveen articulates the military logic of such an alliance, he does little to grapple with the political rationale. Military alliances – formal or otherwise – are a manifestation of political will."

For the most part, this is a fair cop. My essay was largely situated at the level where nations are chess pieces moved about the board, without much thought to the messy business of how political leaders actually get things done. Evan Laksmana's essay in the same issue of Australian Foreign Affairs also offers many sobering arguments for why an Australia–Indonesia military alliance will never happen.

Yet there are two reasons why my proposal might not be as unlikely as it seems. The first is precedent: the Keating–Suharto and Lombok treaties were far-reaching too, which is reason enough to entertain the possibility of an even more ambitious deal.

The second point is that policy can change quickly when circumstances demand it. As I noted in *The Echidna Strategy*, just four days after Russia invaded Ukraine, Germany announced that it would support sanctions to punish Russia, reduce its dependence on Russian energy exports, dramatically boost defence spending and donate weapons to Kyiv. In an instant, Berlin had overturned two decades of accommodationist Russia policy. If Chinese ambitions are as extensive as I fear, then they will inevitably collide with Indonesia's interests, just as Russia's actions collided head-on with Germany's interests. If I'm wrong about China, then little is lost and Australia still benefits from closer ties with Jakarta.

Which brings us to Melissa Conley Tyler's eloquent lament about the indifference towards the bilateral relationship on the Indonesian side. Thinking back on her involvement with Indonesian business, cultural, educational and scientific elites, she feels "a clear sense of Australia becoming less and less relevant". Australia urgently needs to turn this around. We could start with a further boost to higher education scholarships. As Michael Wesley once put it, "education is the cheapest and most effective soft power a country like Australia can deploy". Another objective should be to grow Indonesia's tiny diaspora in Australia by creating a new visa category for Indonesians.

Finally, it's worth noting one practical objection I raised, and which my critics mostly ignored: AUKUS. I think AUKUS materially weakens the prospects for a true strategic partnership with Jakarta because it encourages the very thing South-East Asian leaders tell us they don't want: it turns their region into a theatre for great-power competition, and may even make it a battlefield.

John Blaxland defends AUKUS on the grounds that "weakness invites adventurism". But AUKUS is not the only way to avoid looking weak. Indeed, a security commitment to Indonesia would be a much more effective way to demonstrate strength. Alas, we live in a topsy-turvy world in which buying a fleet of nuclear-powered submarines to fight an enemy 3000 kilometres away is considered the acme of sound strategic policy, whereas advocating for an alliance with a close and powerful neighbour is deemed mildly eccentric.

Sam Roggeveen is the director of the Lowy Institute's International Security Program and author of The Echidna Strategy: Australia's Search for Power and Peace.

Back Issues

ALL PRICES INCLUDE GST,
POSTAGE AND HANDLING.

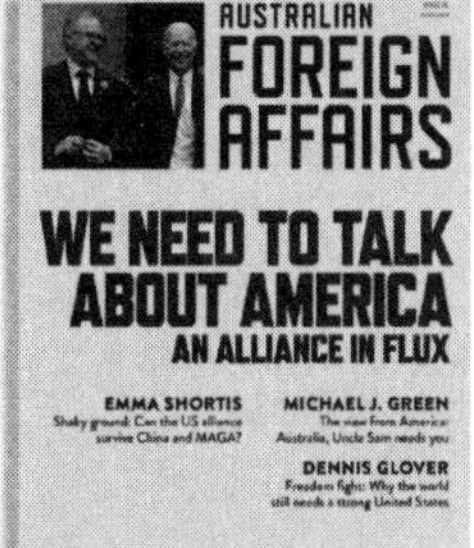

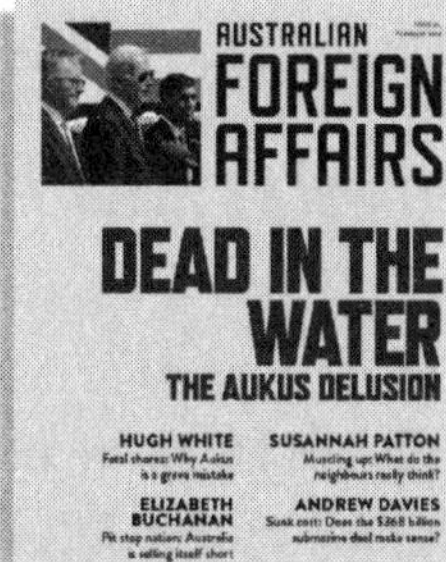

- ☐ **AFA3** ($19.99) Australia & Indonesia
- ☐ **AFA4** ($19.99) Defending Australia
- ☐ **AFA5** ($19.99) Are We Asian Yet?
- ☐ **AFA6** ($19.99) Our Sphere of Influence
- ☐ **AFA7** ($19.99) China Dependence
- ☐ **AFA8** ($19.99) Can We Trust America?
- ☐ **AFA9** ($19.99) Spy vs Spy
- ☐ **AFA10** ($19.99) Friends, Allies and Enemies
- ☐ **AFA11** ($19.99) The March of Autocracy
- ☐ **AFA12** ($19.99) Feeling the Heat
- ☐ **AFA13** ($19.99) India Rising?
- ☐ **AFA14** ($19.99) The Taiwan Choice
- ☐ **AFA15** ($22.99) Our Unstable Neighbourhood
- ☐ **AFA16** ($22.99) The Return of the West
- ☐ **AFA17** ($22.99) Girt by China
- ☐ **AFA18** ($22.99) We need to talk about America
- ☐ **AFA19** ($22.99) Does China really want to attack Australia?
- ☐ **AFA20** ($22.99) The AUKUS Delusion
- ☐ **AFA21** ($24.99) The Jakarta Option

PAYMENT DETAILS I enclose a cheque/money order made out to Schwartz Books Pty Ltd.
Or please debit my credit card (MasterCard, Visa or Amex accepted).

CARD NO. ☐☐☐☐☐☐☐☐☐☐☐☐☐☐☐☐

EXPIRY DATE   /   CCV   AMOUNT $

CARDHOLDER'S NAME

SIGNATURE

NAME

ADDRESS

EMAIL   PHONE

Post or fax this form to: Reply Paid 90094, Collingwood VIC 3066 **Freecall:** 1800 077 514 **or** +61 3 9486 0288
Fax: (03) 9011 6106 **Email:** subscribe@australianforeignaffairs.com **Website:** australianforeignaffairs.com
Subscribe online at australianforeignaffairs.com/subscribe (please do not send electronic scans of this form)

The Back Page

FOREIGN POLICY CONCEPTS AND JARGON, EXPLAINED

THE GLOBAL SOUTH

What is it: A term that groups together developing nations but avoids connotations of poverty associated with predecessors such as "third world", "developing world" and "low- and middle-income countries".

Who coined it: In 1969, Carl Oglesby (anti-war activist and former president, Students for a Democratic Society) coined the term in an article about the Vietnam War, writing that centuries of American "dominance over the Global South ... have converged ... to produce an intolerable social order".

Where is it: Confusingly, the term does not refer to a geographical region. Most poorer countries are in the Southern Hemisphere, especially in Africa and Latin America, but many – including India and China – are not. Joseph Nye (emeritus professor, Harvard) says the term is a political slogan rather than "an accurate description of the world".

Who likes it: Aspiring leaders of the Global South are drawn to the term. Narendra Modi (prime minister, India) claims his country is "becoming the voice of the Global South". In August 2024, Xi Jinping (president, China) told a group of leaders from developing nations that "we are all members of the Global South ... with same ideals and common cause".

Who doesn't: C. Raja Mohan (fellow, Asia Society Policy Institute) believes the term is unhelpful and reductive, saying its flaws emerge "as soon as you scratch even a little bit. What does China have in common with Peru? Qatar with Haiti? Thailand with Sierra Leone? Lumping these countries into a single category ... is a barrier to understanding a complex world."